BLUES
You Can Use
Guitar Chords

BY JOHN GANAPES

ISBN 978-0-7935-6515-3

HAL•LEONARD®
7777 W. BLUEMOUND RD. P.O. BOX 13819 MILWAUKEE, WI 53213

TABLE OF CONTENTS

INTRODUCTION

Who Can Use This Book

The purpose of *Blues You Can Use Guitar Chords* is to give the guitarist a basic understanding of how chords are constructed and to provide an extensive listing of chord forms/voicings relevant to the blues, rhythm 'n' blues (R&B), blues-based rock, and jazz-style blues. These are chords I have found to be useful in playing these styles of music.

Anyone, from beginner to advanced player, who wants to enhance his or her knowledge of chords can benefit from this book. It is not necessary to already have a chord vocabulary.

How to Use This Book

This book has at least two uses. First, it is a chord reference book with which you can discover new chord types and voicings to enhance your chordal playing. Second, it is a basic chord theory book, helping you learn how chords are constructed so you can create your own chords as well as use the ones listed in the book. By learning the theory of chord construction, you can begin to use chords more effectively in both your rhythm and lead playing. However, if you are not interested in the theory, go directly to the CHORD section of this book, which has different chord voicings and their fingerings.

This book is divided into four easy-to-use sections:

I —	THEORY	Chord construction and application
II —	CHORDS	Chord voicings (patterns)
III —	EXERCISES	Exercises and examples designed to help you learn how to use various chords in blues and blues-based music
IV —	APPENDIX	Lists of common chord symbols, scales, chords in various keys, and diagrams designed to show how chords are laid out on the guitar

To obtain the greatest benefit from this book, I suggest the following:

• First, read the chapter that describes a particular chord type (triads, seventh chords, etc.) in the THEORY section. Be sure you understand how chords of that type are constructed.

• Next, go to the CHORD section, and work through the chord voicings given for the chord type about which you just read. This is very important: *be sure to learn each pattern in every position and every key.* When you work through the voicings, drill yourself on the arrangement of the chord members in each pattern. Make sure you know where the root, 3rd, 5th, etc. are located in the pattern.

• After you have learned all the chord voicings in all positions, move on to the EXERCISES section. Work through the examples of chord progressions in the section that corresponds to the chord type you are working on. These sections are clearly marked.

• After you learn a chord progression or exercise, transpose it to all keys. You may have to change the voicings of a given chord type to be able to play a progression comfortably in some keys on the guitar.

• When you feel you have a good grasp of those chords, move on to the next chapter in the THEORY section, and follow through with each chord type.

It is not necessary to spend an excessive amount of time learning each chord type perfectly. Just be sure you have a basic understanding of each type before moving on. Keep practicing the chords you have begun to learn; by working through them this way you'll maximize your results. By the time you've worked through the book you should have a good practical knowledge of chords. Remember this process takes time. Don't expect to absorb everything right away.

The chord diagrams (frames) used in this book follow the standard format you'll find in all of the books of the *BLUES YOU CAN USE* series. The strings run vertically, and the frets run horizontally across the page. The fingerings are given in the first row of numbers at the bottom of the frame. The second row of numbers, which are italicized below the fingerings, indicate the *chord members 1, 3, ♯5, ♭7, etc.*). On top of the frame, Xs and Os indicate which strings to mute and which to sound as open strings, respectively. The fret position, when it is necessary, is indicated by the number at the right of the frame.

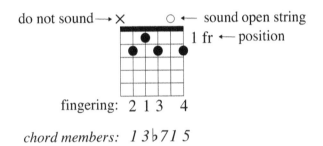

I urge you to explore the fingerboard to search for additional voicings not mentioned here. You may find some you like. Also, this exploring should greatly increase your knowledge of fingerboard harmony. You can't spend too much time learning the fingerboard; only a "second nature" understanding of it will open up your playing and allow your imagination and creative inner self to run free over it.

CHAPTER 1

SOME MUSIC BASICS

Before we begin to construct chords, let's be clear about their rudiments. This is very basic introduction, so if you already know the material presented in a section of this chapter, move on to the next. The first few sections contain fundamental information without which you could not discuss the most basic music theory.

Whole Steps/Half Steps

The distance between notes in music is measured in *whole steps* and *half steps*. A half step is the smallest distance you can move in our musical system (with the exception of smaller quarter-step string bends); a whole step is two half steps.

On the guitar it is very simple: a half step is equal to one fret; a whole step, two frets.

Notes

Notes are given the letter names A, B, C, D, E, F, and G. There are no other letter names used. As you play forward through the alphabet, you are moving *up in pitch*. When you move backwards through the alphabet, you are moving *down in pitch*.

When you move up through this series of notes and get to the top, the note G, the pattern repeats itself, so the next notes up are A, B, C, and so on, one octave higher. Likewise, when you are moving down or backwards through the alphabet and you get to the A, the next notes down are G, F, E, and so on, one octave lower. This chart of the fingerboard should make it all very clear.

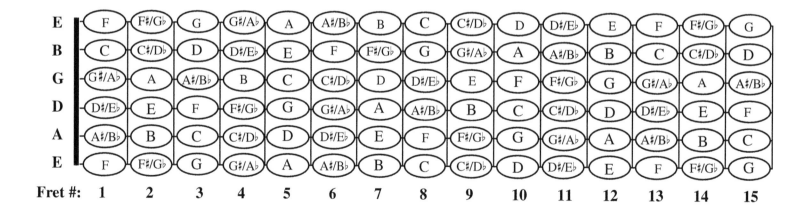

As you can see, some notes have the symbols "♯" and "♭" after them. These symbols are called *accidentals*. Here's what they mean:

♯ is a *sharp* and means you sharp, or raise, a note by one half step.

♭ is a *flat* and means you flat, or lower, a note by one half step.

♮ is a *natural* and means a note is just what the letter name says it is—an "A" note or an "E" note for example—not sharped or flatted. The natural sign is used when a note has been altered in the key signature or somewhere earlier in the bar. A note is assumed to be natural unless otherwise stated.

You'll notice on the fingerboard chart that letter names appear to cover two or three frets next to each other. They also seem to overlap each other, with two note names sometimes sharing the same fret. This is because most of the sharped or flatted notes have more than one name. As an example, look at the sixth string, fourth fret. You'll notice it is one half step above G, which makes it G♯ by the above definitions. But it is also one half step below A, which makes it A♭.

When you have two names for the same pitch, they are called *enharmonic tones*. Which name you choose for the note depends on what key you are in, among other considerations. Don't worry too much about this for now though. We'll see some ways to determine what to call notes in later chapters.

Intervals

Simple Intervals

If you are playing more than one note in a tune (and you most likely are), you are playing intervals—even if you play the same note twice.

An *interval* can be defined as 1) the distance between two notes; or 2) the sound produced by two notes played together.

Intervals fall into two categories: *melodic* and *harmonic*. Melodic intervals are created by notes played sequentially, one after the other, as in a melody. Harmonic intervals are created by notes played simultaneously, both at the same time, as in a chord. We will be dealing with harmonic intervals in this book.

Intervals are identified using numbers. The way to determine an interval's number is based on the letter names of the two notes of the interval. Keeping in mind that we use only the letters A-G for the names of the notes, if you count the letters from one note to another (including the two notes themselves), you will have the number name of the interval.

For example, the interval A to B is the interval of a 2nd, because counting from A to B gives us the number 2 (A=1, B=2; so A to B is a 2nd). As another example, to find the interval from C to A, count C=1, D=2, E=3, F=4, G=5, and A=6. This interval is a 6th.

But what if you have C to E♭, or C to F♯? Well, this brings up the next point.

Intervals can be of three basic types, whether they are melodic or harmonic. Those three types are *major, minor,* and *perfect*. Major is always one half step larger than minor. For example, a minor 2nd is one half step and a major 2nd is two half steps (or one whole step). The intervals of 2nds, 3rds, 6ths, and 7ths can be major or minor. The intervals of unisons, 4ths, 5ths, and octaves (8ths) can only be one size (with a few exceptions that you'll see in a moment) and are called perfect intervals.

Here is a list of intervals with C as their starting, or bottom, note:

Unison	0 half steps	C to C (the same note)
Minor 2nd	1 half step	C to D♭
Major 2nd	2 half steps	C to D
Minor 3rd	3 half steps	C to E♭
Major 3rd	4 half steps	C to E
Diminished 4th	4 half steps	C to F♭
Perfect 4th	5 half steps	C to F
Augmented 4th	6 half steps	C to F♯
Diminished 5th	6 half steps	C to G♭
Perfect 5th	7 half steps	C to G
Augmented 5th	8 half steps	C to G♯
Minor 6th	8 half steps	C to A♭
Major 6th	9 half steps	C to A
Minor 7th	10 half steps	C to B♭
Major 7th	11 half steps	C to B
Octave (8th)	12 half steps	C to C (the next C up)

Notice there is an augmented 4th listed in the above chart. Any perfect or major interval can be *augmented* (made larger by one half step). You can also find an interval labeled "diminished 5th" right below the augmented 4th. Any perfect or minor interval may also be *diminished* (made smaller by one half step).

If you look at the above chart, you'll see that with the exception of the augmented 4th (C to F♯) and the augmented 5th (C to G♯), there are only flats (♭) and no sharps (♯). The F♯ is used because if a G♭ were used instead, the interval could not be called an augmented 4th. By the system we are using, C to G♭ would be a kind of 5th (five letter names: C–D–E–F–G). More specifically, it would be a diminished 5th, which is, as you can see on the above chart, the same number of half steps as an augmented 4th. The two intervals, C to F♯ and C to G♭, sound the same since they are the same pitches.

While you can augment or diminish any of the intervals, we don't want to get too complicated in this book. Most often only 4ths and 5ths are augmented or diminished because they are perfect intervals, and that's all we're going to cover here.

Compound Intervals

There are intervals larger than an octave. They are called *compound intervals* and are made up of a combination of an octave and some smaller interval. We will be using some of the following compound intervals.

Minor 9th	octave + minor 2nd	C to D♭ in the next octave range
Major 9th	octave + major 2nd	C to D in the next octave range
Minor 10th	octave + minor 3rd	C to E♭ in the next octave range
Major 10th	octave + major 3rd	C to E in the next octave range
Perfect 11th	octave + perfect 4th	C to F in the next octave range
Perfect 12th	octave + perfect 5th	C to G in the next octave range
Minor 13th	octave + minor 6th	C to A♭ in the next octave range
Major 13th	octave + major 6th	C to A in the next octave range

The following illustration shows all of the above intervals on the guitar.

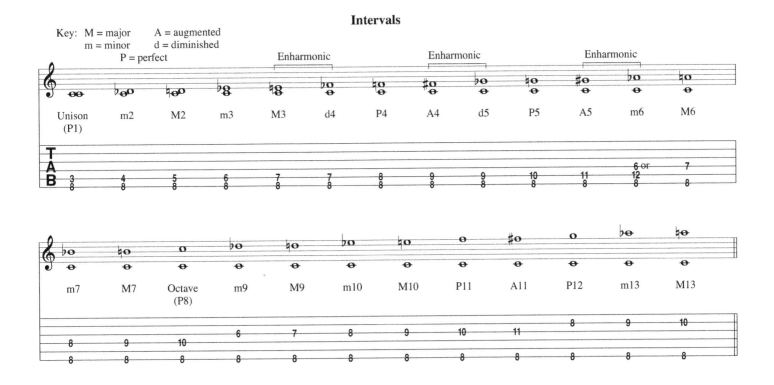

There are also 14ths (an octave plus a 7th), but we don't use them to make chords. In fact we won't be using 10ths or 12ths either. They're listed just to show how compound intervals work.

While we've been looking at intervals from the perspective of moving up from a bottom note, you can also look at intervals from the other perspective—moving down from a top note. When building chords though, we usually look at them from the bottom up. We'll be looking at constructing chords using intervals as building blocks, but we'll also consider other ways of looking at chords.

Try playing the various intervals on the guitar to get a feel for how they sound and how they lie on the fingerboard. Find each of the above types all over the neck, using different notes as the bottom reference note. Play up from a note, and play down from it as well.

This is not just a theoretical exercise. As you learn how different intervals sound and associate them with patterns on the fingerboard, you will be able to play the ideas you hear in your head with greater ease, because you will know which intervals to play.

Basic Scale Theory

Before discussing harmony, we need to review a little scale theory.

All scales in Western music use the letter names A, B, C, D, E, F, and G, as you saw in the Notes section. Some scales have less than seven notes and don't use all of the letter names, of course, but the ones we will be using are seven-note scales and include all notes, A through G. No other letter names are used.

When discussing the notes of a scale, each note is given a number. The *root* is the first note of the scale, and so it gets the number 1.

> The *root* of a scale is the bottom note, which shares the same name as the key (C major scale/C is the root; E minor scale/E is the root).

The rest of the notes of the scale are numbered in order, up to 7. The following illustration shows the notes of the C major scale with their *scale degree numbers*.

> *Scale degree* is another name for each individual note of the scale.

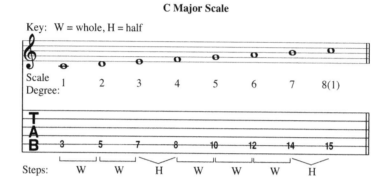

The intervals between each of the notes in the scale are indicated in the above illustration. All major scales share the same pattern of intervals. Starting with the root, or scale degree 1, the pattern is as follows: scale degree 1 to 2 (whole step, or two frets), 2 to 3 (whole step), 3 to 4 (half step, or one fret), 4 to 5 (whole step), 5 to 6 (whole step), 6 to 7 (whole step), and 7 to 8 (half step).

In the key of C major, all of the notes are natural; there are no sharped or flatted notes. When changing to other keys, however, we have to *alter* one or more of these notes.

> *Alter*, in this case, means to sharp or flat a note—to raise it or lower it by one half step (one fret).

So, in the key of C, the notes are C–D–E–F–G–A–B, all natural notes. In the key of G, the F must be raised one half step (one fret) to F♯. The notes of the G major scale are (starting with the note that has the same name as the key) G–A–B–C–D–E–F♯. Likewise, in the key of F, we have to lower the B to B♭. The F major scale consists of the notes F–G–A–B♭–C–D–E. The notes of each of the twelve major and twelve minor scales are given in the APPENDIX.

Minor scales work in a similar way to major scales. The only difference is in the pattern of intervals. The natural minor scale, which we will use to build minor chords, has the following pattern: 1 to 2 (whole step), 2 to 3 (half step), 3 to 4 (whole step), 4 to 5 (whole step), 5 to 6 (half step), 6 to 7 (whole step), and 7 to 8 (whole step).

Along with the different interval pattern, there are different altered notes in the minor scale of a given key. In the C natural minor scale, for example, the notes aren't all natural. We still use the letter names C, D, E, F, G, A, and B—but E, A, and B are flatted. So the notes of the C natural minor scale are C–D–E♭–F–G–A♭–B♭. Here's what it looks like.

C Natural Minor Scale

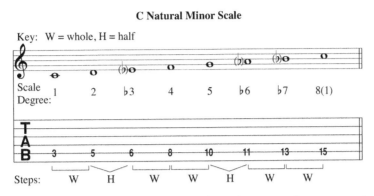

In relation to the major scale, the minor scale contains ♭3rd, ♭6th, and ♭7th scale degrees. We will use both major and natural minor scales in one method of building our chords. It will be an alternative way of looking at them, in addition to the intervallic method mentioned in the previous section on intervals.

Tertian Harmony

In most Western music, the type of harmonic (chordal) system used is *tertian harmony*. In this system, chords are built in intervals of 3rds.

As you will remember from the section on intervals, there are two types of 3rds—one made up of three half steps, the other of four. If the 3rd is made up of three half steps, it is called a *minor 3rd*. If it is made up of four half steps, it is called a *major 3rd*.

You can think of a 3rd as being every *other* note of a major or minor scale. This is how we are going to look at the chord construction. To build a chord, simply use every other note of the major or minor scale, starting with the root, or scale degree 1.

Since we skip scale degree numbers 2, 4, and 6 (with a couple of exceptions we'll look at in later chapters) we need a way to use those notes in our system. The solution is simple: we use a two-octave scale. That way we get scale degrees 1, 3, 5, and 7 from the first octave, and then, skipping the root (scale degree 1) of the second octave, we get 2, 4, and 6 from the second octave. After that, the cycle repeats itself. (We end up back at the root, or 1.)

When we use a note from the second octave, we add 7 to its scale degree number to get the name of the *chord member*. (This is because the first octave has seven notes.)

Chord member is just another name for a note of a chord.

C13 Chord Derived from C Major Scale
(The 7th degree, B, is flatted)

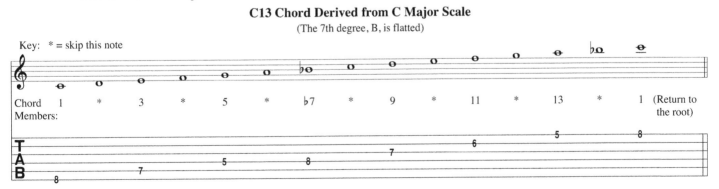

As you add more and more notes to make bigger chords—such as ninths and thirteenths—you'll find them very difficult if not impossible to play anywhere on the guitar. Fortunately, we don't need to play all the notes of those chords; some of the less important notes may be left out without significantly changing the sound and function of the chord. As we study each chord type, we'll discuss which notes may be omitted without changing the character of a chord.

The notes of a chord may be rearranged and do not have to be stacked in order. In fact, on the guitar it becomes very difficult to play larger, extended chords without shuffling the notes around so they fit within a shorter range of frets on the fingerboard.

The following example shows the difficulty you can encounter when you try to play a C9 chord without rearranging the notes, as well as a possible solution to the problem.

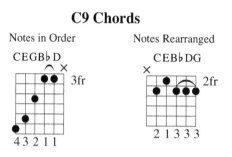

C9 Chords

There are many types of chords that can be used in blues-based music. In this book, we will construct triads (major, minor, diminished, and augmented), seventh chords, sixth chords, ninth chords, eleventh chords, thirteenth chords, and altered versions of these chords.

The I-IV-V Blues Progression

Most often, the chords in this book will be given in the context of the basic I-IV-V blues chord progression. Very simply, the roman numerals refer to the scale degree which is the root of a given chord. We use roman numerals so we know we're talking about the root of a chord and how it "fits" in a key. (We call this a chord's *function*.)

So, if you build a chord which has as its root the first note of the scale of the given key, it's called a *I chord*. If you build a chord which has as its root the fourth note of the scale, it's a *IV chord*. If you build a note which has as its root the fifth note of the scale, it's a *V chord*. This is where we get the roman numeral names. You can build a chord on any note of the scale.

A listing of the I, IV, and V chords, as well as other chords in the blues keys, major keys, and minor keys, is given in the APPENDIX.

For a more detailed explanation of blues progressions, see the first book of this series, *Blues You Can Use*.

CHAPTER 2

TRIADS

The smallest and most basic chord you can build is a *triad*, or three-note chord.

A *chord* is three or more different notes played as one unit.

There are four different types of triads—major, minor, diminished, and augmented. All chords in tertian harmony contain some type of triad. Any other type of chord (seventh, ninth, etc.) has the same character as the basic triad which it contains (major, minor, etc.).

Major Triads

Building From Scales

Building a major triad is very simple. You saw in the tertian harmony lesson in Chapter 1 that we use every other note of the scale to build chords. To build a major chord of any kind, then, we simply use a major scale to find our notes.

Starting with the first note of the scale as the root of the chord, skip the second degree of the scale and move on to the third degree, making that the 3rd of the chord. Then skip the fourth degree, and use the fifth degree of the scale for the 5th of the chord (the final note of the triad).

To get a C major chord, use a C major scale. To get a G major chord, use a G major scale. It will work this way for any chord. Just use the major scale with the same name as the chord you want to build. The first part of the following diagram illustrates this:

C Major Triad

You can see that the notes of a C major chord are C, E, and G, or 1, 3, and 5, respectively.

The Intervallic View

Look at the right side of the above diagram (labeled "Intervallic View"). You can see that the interval between the root and 3rd of the major triad is a major 3rd. The interval between the 3rd and 5th of the chord is a minor 3rd. So we have a major 3rd on the bottom and a minor 3rd on the top. The outside interval formed between the root and the 5th is a perfect 5th.

Major triads can be used as I, IV, or V chords in the blues, but most often you will turn them into sevenths, ninths, or other extended chords, as we'll see in the next chapters. Major triads are used extensively though in rock and R&B styles, again most often as I, IV, or V chords.

Minor Triads

Building From Scales

Minor triads are built exactly the same way as major triads but with one important difference—we use a different scale. Just as we used a major scale to build any type of major chord, we use a natural minor scale to build any kind of minor chord. Here is a C minor triad built from the C natural minor scale.

C Minor Triad

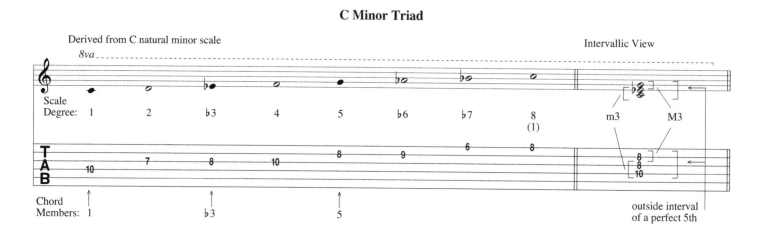

Here you can see the C minor triad contains the notes C, E♭, and G for the 1, 3, and 5 of the chord. Notice the only difference between a major triad and a minor triad of the same name (in this case C) is the 3rd of the chord. The C major has an E♮ for the 3rd and the C minor has an E♭. Since we are relating all notes to the major scale, we say the minor triad has a *flatted 3rd*.

Since the 3rd of the chord is the only note that tells us whether the chord is major or minor, it is a very important note in triads and their extensions (seventh chords, ninth chords, etc.). We'll see later how this knowledge comes in very handy when building chords.

The Intervallic View

The stack of 3rds in a minor triad is reverse that of a major triad. Look at the "Intervallic View" in the above diagram. You can see that now the minor 3rd is on the *bottom*, and the major 3rd is on top of it. The larger, outside interval formed by both stacks of 3rds is the same, however—a perfect 5th.

Minor triads are used in the same way as major triads, but in minor keys. They can also be used as secondary chords in a major key, which is explained thoroughly in *Blues You Can Use*. The secondary chords in all keys are listed here in the APPENDIX.

Diminished Triads

The simplest way to build a diminished triad is to take a *minor triad*, and *flat the 5th*—lowering the 5th of the chord one half step (one fret). Using the C minor triad we just built, we'll lower the G (5 of the C minor chord) and make it a G♭ (♭5). Here it is.

C Diminished Triad
Derived from a C minor triad

Looking at the diminished chord as a stack of intervals, we see it's made up of a minor 3rd on the bottom and a minor 3rd on the top. The larger interval made up of the two minor 3rds is a *diminished 5th*. Remember from the Intervals section in Chapter 1 that to diminish an interval is to lower it by one half step.

The diminished triad functions in a fairly unusual way in a blues progression. Usually it's not actually a chord of the key. More often it's used as a *passing chord* which "passes" from one chord in the key to another. It makes the chord movement stronger or smoother, or both. As with the major and minor triads, diminished chords are most often made into seventh chords for use in the blues. We'll see how to use them a little later in this book.

Augmented Triads

Augmented triads can be built as easily as diminished triads. However, in this case you start with a *major triad* and *sharp the 5th*. Remember sharping a note means to raise it one half step. So if we take the C major triad we built earlier in this chapter and raise the 5th—which is G—we end up with G♯ as the 5th of the chord, making it an augmented chord. In other words, an augmented triad is a major triad with a *sharp, or raised, 5th*.

C Augmented Triad
Derived from a C major triad

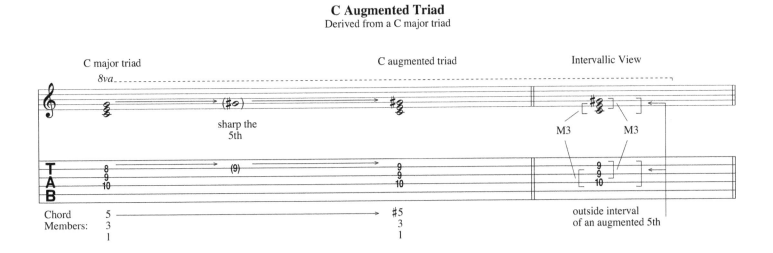

Intervallically speaking, augmented triads are made up of a major 3rd on the bottom and a major 3rd on the top. They stack up together to make an *augmented 5th* for the larger, outside interval.

Augmented chords are most often used as the V chord in a blues progression. They have a very distinctive sound as you'll hear when you work through them. They stand out and make the chord progression stronger when used in moderation. They are usually found at the end of the chord progression, making the return to the top of the cycle (or end of the song) stand out.

Inversions

The root does not have to be the bottom, or *bass note*, of a chord form. When it is in the bass, the chord is said to be in *root position*. However, any one of the other notes of the chord can be in the bass. If a note other than the root is in the bass, it is called an *inversion*. If the 3rd of the chord is in the bass, it is called *first inversion*. If the 5th of the chord is in the bass, it is called *second inversion*. This may be a bit complicated at first, but you'll get used to it as you work with the chords in this book.

The inversion of a chord is very important to its sound. Sometimes if you play a song with the correct chord but the wrong inversion, it doesn't sound right. This is because the inversion gives a song its own individual feel. The highest and lowest notes in a chord (top and bottom notes) are the ones that stand out the most, and so they most often define the character of a particular voicing. Every type of chord can be inverted, from triads and seventh chords through thirteenths. You'll hear the difference as you work through the chord inversions in the CHORDS section of this book. The inversions will be indicated in most of the diagrams.

Doubling

Here's one final note before we move on to the chord diagrams. You saw that a triad is made up of only three notes, but does this mean you can only use three strings to play a major or minor triad? The answer is *no*.

You can *double* any or all of the notes. By this we mean you can play the root, 3rd, or 5th of a triad (or any note of a chord, for that matter) in two or more places. The doubled notes will be an octave or two apart and will only count as one note because their function is the same within the chord. (Remember the definition of a chord is *three or more different notes*.)

Doubling lets you build a fuller sounding chord. You'll see sometimes you can have the same note on three different strings in a chord. This is still called doubling even though it is actually tripled.

The following illustration shows an E major chord played with just three notes and no doubling, followed by another E major chord with the root played on three different strings in three different octaves, and the 5th of the chord played on two strings an octave apart. They are the same chord, but when you play them you will hear a big difference in the sound.

E Major Chords

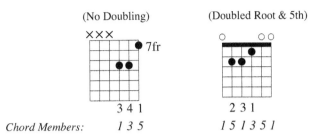

(No Doubling)

(Doubled Root & 5th)

7fr

Chord Members:

3 4 1

1 3 5

2 3 1

1 5 1 3 5 1

Now go to the CHORDS section of this book and look over the triad voicings given there. There are quite a few, and I encourage you to study them all carefully. Triads are the basis for the rest of the chords in this book. Learn them all over the fingerboard, using every note as the root. Play each chord in each position as a major, minor, diminished, and augmented triad. (For the most part they are laid out that way.)

After you have thoroughly practiced triads as described above, go on to the EXERCISES section to see some of the ways they can be used.

CHAPTER 3

SEVENTH CHORDS

Triads are the basic building blocks in tertian harmony. We saw in the last chapter that you use the 1st, 3rd, and 5th degrees of a scale to build a triad. To build a seventh chord, simply add the 7th scale degree on top of this triad. You end up with the 1st, 3rd, 5th, and 7th scale degrees in your chord.

You can use any of the four types of triads to make a seventh chord. In this chapter we'll build seventh chords using only the major and minor triads—making major seventh, dominant seventh, and minor seventh chords. We'll look at how to build seventh chords with diminished and augmented triads in later chapters.

Major Seventh Chords

Building From Scales

Since major sevenths are *major* sounding chords, we'll use a major scale to find their component notes. In the following example, we'll build a C major seventh chord from the C major scale. We'll use the 1st, 3rd, and 5th scale degrees for the 1, 3, and 5 of our chord, skip the 6th scale degree, and use the 7th degree to make the 7th of the chord.

C Major Seventh Chord

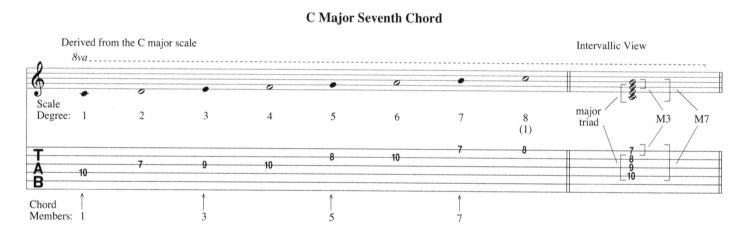

You can see that a C major seventh chord is made up of the notes C, E, G, and B—for the 1, 3, 5, and 7 of the chord, respectively—all taken straight and unaltered from the C major scale.

The Intervallic View

Looking at the right side of the above illustration, you can see that a major seventh chord is made up of a major triad (a major 3rd on the bottom and a minor 3rd on top) with a major 3rd on top of it. The larger, outer interval formed by this stack of three 3rds is a *major 7th*.

Major seventh chords are not used a great deal in the blues except for jazz-style blues, where they are often used for the I and IV chords. They are also used in a fair amount of more modern rock and especially in R&B tunes. I'm sure you'll recognize their sound.

You'll find if you play against a major seventh chord using a scale which has a *flat 7th* in it, which most blues scales do, it will clash very strongly with the natural 7th in the chord. In playing against a major seventh chord, you're restricted to using either a major scale, a mode or scale with the natural 7th in it, or a scale that has no 7th in it at all, like the *major pentatonic scale* described in detail in *Blues You Can Use*.

Dominant Seventh Chords

Building From Scales

Dominant seventh chords can be built very easily by taking a major seventh chord and *flatting the 7th*. Though sometimes called major-minor seventh chords because they are a major triad with a minor seventh as the outside interval, we'll refer to them as dominant sevenths throughout this book. Here's how to build a C dominant seventh chord:

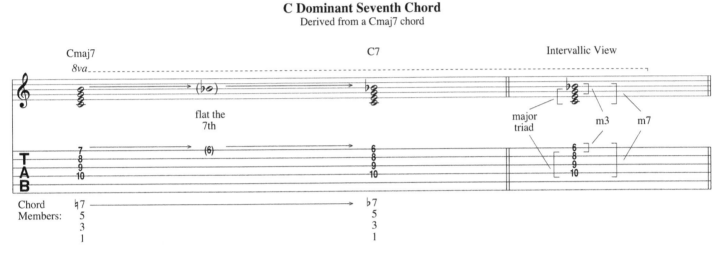

C Dominant Seventh Chord
Derived from a Cmaj7 chord

The notes are C, E, G, and B♭ for the 1, 3, 5, and ♭7 of the chord, respectively.

The Intervallic View

This chord stacks up as a major triad (a major 3rd on the bottom and a minor 3rd on the top) with a minor 3rd on top. As indicated above, the outer interval is a minor 7th.

Dominant seventh chords are used extensively in the blues as well as in rock, R&B, and jazz. In a blues progression, they can be used for the I, IV, and V chords. They give a little more "bite" than plain major and minor chords.

Minor Seventh Chords

Building From Scales

Minor seventh chords are built the same way as major sevenths are, just using the natural minor scale instead of the major scale. We'll look at the construction of a C minor seventh chord in the following example. Notice that the 3rd and 7th degrees of the scale are flatted, giving you a 1, ♭3, 5, and ♭7 for the notes of the chord.

C Minor Seventh Chord

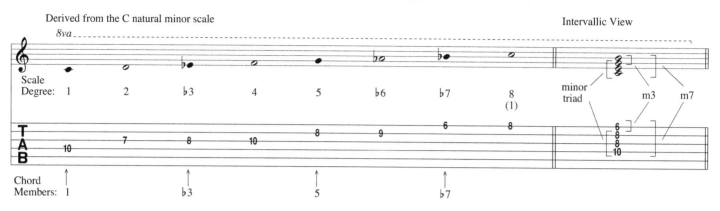

The notes of the C minor seventh chord are C, E♭, G, and B♭ for the 1, ♭3, 5, and ♭7 of the chord, respectively.

The Intervallic View

Intervallically, the minor seventh chord is a minor triad (a minor 3rd on the bottom and a major 3rd on top) with a minor 3rd on top, as the above diagram illustrates.

Minor seventh chords can be used for the i, iv, and v chords in minor blues progressions, and for other chords in major keys, as we'll see later in this book. They're used extensively in rock, R&B, and jazz, as well as in the blues. (Note: When we refer to a minor chord by its roman numeral, we use a lower case letter. We don't have to call it a "minor I," because the lower case "i" tells us it's a minor chord.)

You'll notice the only difference between minor seventh and dominant seventh chords is the 3rd, just as it is with triads. Again you can see that the 3rd of the chord is an extremely important note. In fact, if you were to omit the root and 5th of the chord, it would still be heard as a seventh chord in the context of the chord progression—especially if the bass provided the root.

All seventh chords can be played as inversions, just as triads can. But in this case there is one more inversion, since there is one more note in the chord. The inversions are as follows: if the root is in the bass, the chord is in *root position*; if the 3rd is in the bass, the chord is in *first inversion*; if the 5th is in the bass, it's in *second inversion*; and if the 7th is in the bass, it's in *third inversion*.

Third inversion seventh chords sound like they want to *resolve*, or move to the next chord, in very specific ways. Listen carefully when you attempt to use them and be sure you're not creating *tension* without clearly *resolving* it. Usually the bass note (which is the 7th of the chord in this inversion) wants to move down one half or one whole step. If the next chord allows this, great. If not, it may sound unresolved.

Now go to the CHORDS section and work through the seventh chords in the same way that you did with the triads. This time, the voicings are laid out with the major seventh, dominant seventh, and minor seventh chords together in the same position and inversion, so you can see clearly on the fingerboard which notes change with different types of seventh chords and which ones stay the same.

If you are strictly interested in the blues, you can just work on the dominant seventh and minor seventh chords for now. Those are the seventh chords you'll most often hear in strict blues style. However, I strongly encourage you to learn them all particularly if you are interested in any other type of music, including jazz-style blues.

CHAPTER 4
DIMINISHED SEVENTH CHORDS

Among the chords we are studying in this book, diminished seventh chords are unique in two ways. First, because of the way they are constructed intervallically—they're made up of a diminished triad with a minor 3rd on top which creates a *double-flatted seventh* (♭♭7th). Since there are twelve notes (twelve half steps) to an octave, and minor 3rds are made up of three half steps, the octave is divided up evenly by the four notes of the chord (4 x 3 frets = 12 frets). Thanks to this unique interval structure, the same fingering shape can be used for each inversion of the chord, simply by moving the shape up the fingerboard three frets at a time. Examine the following diagram to see how this works.

C Diminished Seventh Chord

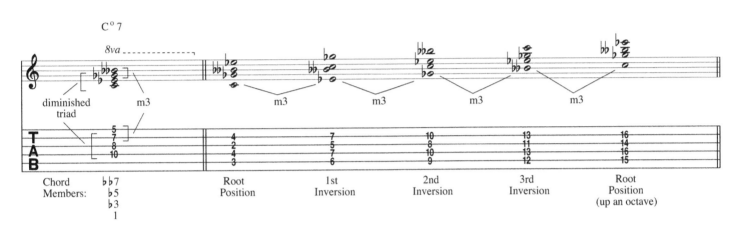

The second unique quality of diminished seventh chords is that, due to the way they are symmetrically constructed, *any one of the four notes in the chord can be the root!* A diminished seventh chord made up of the notes C, E♭, G♭, and B♭♭ can be a C dim7, E♭ dim7, G♭ dim7, or B♭♭ dim7 (which we'll call Adim7). The reason we use a B♭♭ note (and not an A) in the chord is we have to build our chords with 3rds, so we need to use every other letter name to spell them. You could, for example, "re-spell" G♭dim7 to make it an F♯ dim7 (using the enharmonic notes F♯, A, C, and E♭). Just remember to use every other letter name and flat or sharp them, if necessary, to make intervals of minor 3rds. Look at the following illustration to see how it works.

Enharmonic Spellings of a Diminished Seventh Chord

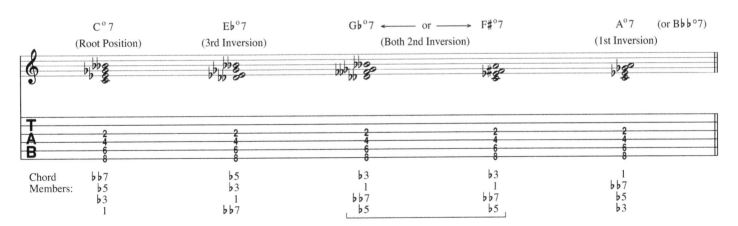

Of course, this can get to be quite complicated and confusing. Don't worry too much about it. All you really have to remember is the diminished seventh chord you play must contain the root of the chord you want. The rest of the notes will be correct.

The above characteristics of the diminished seventh chord make it a very flexible chord to use in terms of voicings. On the other hand, there are not a lot of places where you find a use for it in blues-based music. One of the most common uses is as a *passing chord*, when moving from a IV to a I chord. Another is as a substitute for a V chord, using the diminished chord based on the ♮7th degree of the scale. We'll see examples of how to use diminished seventh chords in these ways, as well as others, in the EXERCISES section. First go to the CHORDS section to get the voicings. Because of the repetitive nature of the chord, there aren't many different fingering patterns.

CHAPTER 5
SIXTH CHORDS

Sixth chords are a little different from the chords we've looked at so far because they can be major or minor but not dominant. They can be interchanged with some dominant chords in the blues, but by themselves they don't function as such. They are also different because we don't build them entirely from 3rds. Sixth chords are major or minor triads with the sixth scale degree added on top. The chord tones are the root, 3rd, 5th, and 6th. The 6th is an interval of a major 2nd (one whole step) above the 5th, instead of the interval of a 3rd.

Major Sixth Chords

Building From Scales

To build a major sixth chord, we again use the major scale (because we're building a major type of chord). After constructing a major triad with the 1st, 3rd, and 5th scale degrees, we put the 6th degree of the scale on top. The following diagram shows the construction of a C major sixth chord.

C Major Sixth Chord

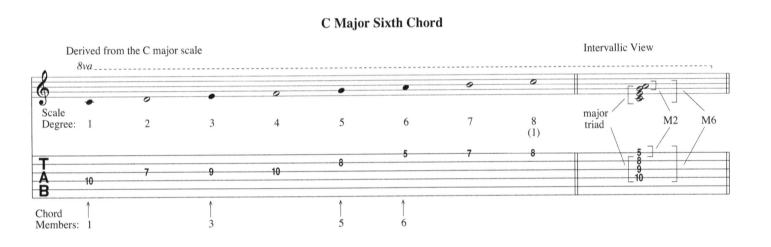

It's pretty simple, as you can see. The notes of a C major sixth chord are C, E, G, and A.

The Intervallic View

The major sixth chord is constructed from a major triad (major 3rd on the bottom, minor 3rd on top) and a major 2nd (one whole step) placed on top of the chord. The outside interval is a major 6th. Look at the above illustration to see how it works.

Major sixth chords are often referred to as *color chords* because they add harmonic *color* to a tune. They can be used as the I and IV chords in twelve-bar blues and are also used extensively in jazz and jazz-style blues, as well as in R&B tunes. In jazz and R&B settings, they are often alternated with major seventh chords. In twelve-bar blues, they are often alternated with dominant seventh and ninth chords, even though they are not technically dominant chords.

Minor Sixth Chords

Building From Scales

The way to build a minor sixth chord is to use the 1st, ♭3rd, 5th, and 6th degrees of the natural minor scale. Remember that the 6th degree is flatted (♭6) in a natural minor scale. We raise it to make a natural 6th (♮6). This prevents it from clashing with the 5th of the chord, only a half step away from the ♭6th. In the key of C minor, for instance, we have an A♭ for the 6th degree. We have to raise it one half step to an A♮. That means that the 6th of the chord is one whole step above the 5th—just like in the major sixth chord. Here's what a C minor sixth chord looks like:

C Minor Sixth Chord

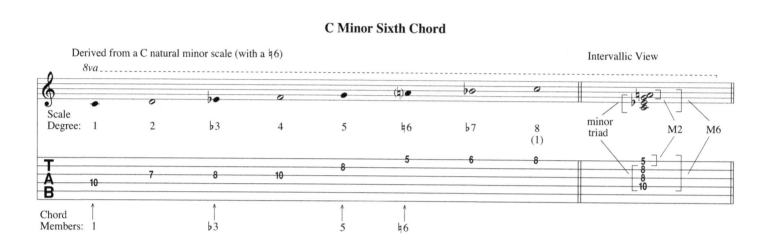

The notes of the C minor sixth chord are C, E♭, G and A♮.

The Intervallic View

By now, you probably know what the stack of intervals in a minor sixth chord is. The bottom contains a minor triad with the interval of a minor 3rd below a major 3rd. On top we put the interval of a major 2nd. The above illustration makes this clear.

Minor sixth chords are again used for harmonic color, and are alternated with minor seventh and ninth chords. They are beautiful chords and can be used wherever any of the previously discussed minor chords can. The key to their use lies in the individual player's ear. If you like the sound, use it. After all, it is through the use of unusual, "odd," or "wrong" chords that the frontiers of music are expanded outward. Today's norm was likely considered improper form at one time or another.

Look at the voicings given in the CHORDS section, then work through the EXERCISES section. Finally, play around with them in a blues setting—as well as in any other setting you like. See how you like them.

CHAPTER 6

NINTH CHORDS

We saw in the last chapter how seventh chords are constructed. They had as their basis a major or minor triad with the 7th added. In this chapter we will see that ninth chords are in fact an *extension* of seventh chords. *Every ninth chord contains a seventh chord.* Furthermore, every ninth chord functions the same as its equivalent seventh chord—major, minor, or dominant—and can be used in place of that type of seventh chord. This will hold true for all of the *extended chords* that we'll look at in the following chapters.

Just as there are three basic types of seventh chords, there are also three basic types of ninth chords—major, minor, and dominant. We determine the type of ninth chord by the type of seventh chord it contains.

In the tertian harmony section, we learned that seventh chords are made up of the 1st, 3rd, 5th, and 7th degrees of the scale and that those notes are all contained in the *first octave* of that scale. We also learned to be able to continue building a chord from this scale—still skipping every other note—we have to use a *two-octave scale*. The 9th is the first note of the second octave of this scale. This is true for major or minor sounding ninth chords.

Major Ninth Chords

Building From Scales

To build a major ninth chord, first build a major seventh chord using the 1st, 3rd, 5th, and 7th degrees of the major scale, as we did in the last chapter. Then skip the root in the second octave, and use the 2nd scale degree, putting it on the top of the chord. Remember from the tertian harmony lesson that when we use notes from the second octave of a scale, we add 7 to its scale degree number to get the *chord member number*. In this case, we add 7 + 2 and get 9. So the note we get is the 9th of the chord. Here's what it looks like in the key of C major. (We'll have to start with the root on the sixth string—an octave lower than in the previous chapters—in order to get a full two-octave scale.)

C Major Ninth Chord

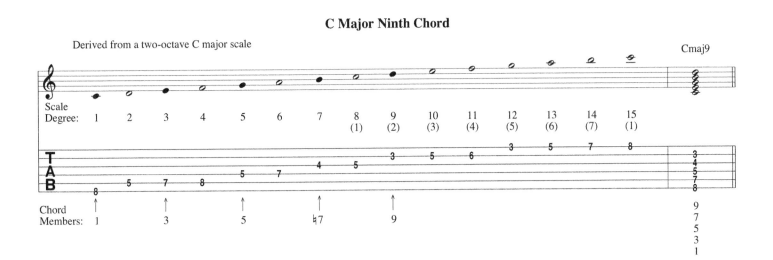

The notes of the C major ninth chord are C, E, G, B, and D and are the 1, 3, 5, 7, and 9 of the chord, respectively.

The Intervallic View

The intervallic view reveals a major seventh chord on the bottom (a major 3rd with a minor 3rd on top of it, and a major 3rd on top of that), and a minor 3rd on top, making the full ninth chord. The large, outside interval is a major 9th, a compound interval.

C Major Ninth Chord

Intervallic View

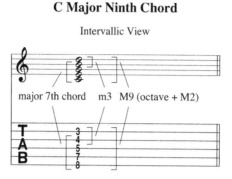

major 7th chord   m3   M9 (octave + M2)

Major ninth chords, like major seventh chords, are not used much in the blues, except in jazz-style blues. They are used in some R&B tunes and can be used very effectively in some ballad-type rock tunes. Jimi Hendrix made beautiful use of them in some of his earlier, psychedelic work.

Dominant Ninth Chords

Building From Scales

Dominant ninth chords are formed by taking a dominant seventh chord and adding the 9th scale degree to it. The 9th we add is the same 9th we used in the major ninth chord and comes from the same scale. The only difference between a dominant ninth and major ninth chord is the quality of the 7th. A dominant seventh chord has a *flatted 7th*. In a C dominant ninth chord (C9) the notes are C, E, G, B♭, and D, which constitute the 1, 3, 5, ♭7, and 9 of the chord.

C Dominant Ninth Chord

Derived from Cmaj9 chord

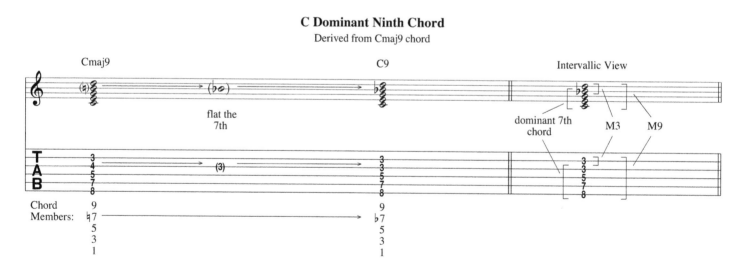

The Intervallic View

The 3rds in a ninth chord stack up like this: On the bottom there is a major triad, on top of that there is a minor 3rd (making a dominant seventh chord), and on top of that is a major 3rd. The outside interval is still a major 9th. The right side of the above illustration demonstrates this.

Dominant ninths are used extensively in all kinds of blues and R&B tunes. They also are used, to some degree, in rock. They can be used anywhere a dominant seventh chord can be used, which is for the I, IV, or V chord, and generally offer a "smoother," more sophisticated sound than the seventh chord.

As with seventh chords, whenever we refer to a chord as just a ninth chord, with no indication of major or minor before it, we assume it to be a dominant ninth chord.

Minor Ninth Chords

Building From Scales

Minor ninth chords have as their basis a *minor seventh chord*. We build a minor ninth chord the same way we built the major ninth chords, only we use the natural minor scale. Here's how you construct a C minor ninth chord:

C Minor Ninth Chord

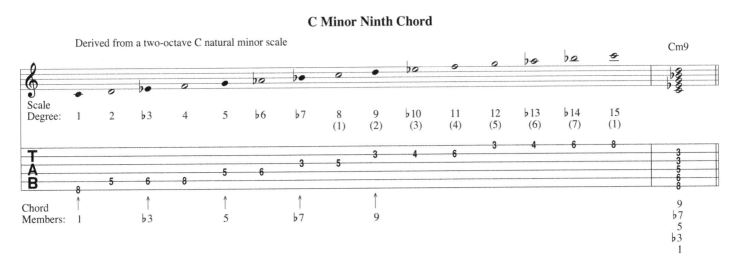

The notes of the C minor ninth chord are C, E♭, G, B♭ and D—for the 1, ♭3, 5, ♭7, and 9 of the chord, respectively. For all three ninth chords based on C we use a D natural (D♮) for the 9th of the chord. This is because the 2nd scale degree is the same note in both major and minor scales.

The Intervallic View

Minor ninth chords contain a minor seventh chord. On top of that we stack a major 3rd to complete the chord. The interval stack is, from the bottom up: minor 3rd, major 3rd, minor 3rd, major 3rd. The outside interval is a major 9th.

C Minor Ninth Chord

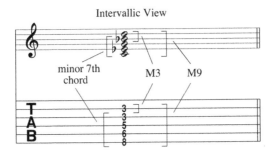

Minor ninths are used in the blues, especially jazz style, as well as in R&B and some rock. They are beautiful chords, and can give you a big, smooth sound. However, they don't fit everywhere. In a basic minor blues progression they can be used for the i and iv chords. I don't find them as useful as a v chord because the 9th of that chord is not in the minor scale and clashes with it. They can also be used in an *embellished* blues progression as *secondary chords* (i.e., the ii, iii, and vi chords). You'll find examples of this in the EXERCISES section of this book. (For more information, see *Blues You Can Use*.) Try them anywhere you find minor seventh chords.

Ninth chords also may be inverted, just like seventh chords. When the root is in the bass the chord is in *root position*. When the 3rd is in the bass it is a *first inversion* chord. With the 5th in the bass it is a *second inversion* chord, and with the 7th in the bass it is a *third inversion* chord. The 9th may also be in the bass, but this is less common. You have to use your ear in such a situation because these particular inversons are considered "unstable," and don't work in all settings. Most often you would use one to pass quickly between two more "stable" inversions.

As you know by now, we usually don't stack the notes of an extended chord in order (1–3–5–7–9). The finger stretch would be too great for most of us, and many of the patterns would require an extra finger! We have to arrange them so they fit within a smaller range on the fingerboard.

When stacking the notes of a ninth chord, it is usually best to place the 7th of the chord *below* the 9th, as this results in a better sound. Of course, no rule of harmony is absolute, but to some degree, various styles dictate what is acceptable.

As with seventh chords, certain notes of ninth chords are more important than others. The essential notes are the 3rd, 7th, and 9th of the chord. As you will remember, the 3rd tells us whether a chord is major or minor. The 7th must be included along with the 9th because, without it, the chord would be an *add 9 chord*. (We will look at *add 9* chords in a later chapter.) However, the root and 5th may both be omitted without affecting the quality of the chord (major, minor, or dominant). In fact, most ninth chord voicings do omit one or the other. Full ninth chord voicings are very lush and can be too full for group playing.

You can use voicings which don't contain the 3rd of the chord if someone else is supplying it or if you immediately move to another voicing which does contain it.

Turn to the CHORDS section, and learn the ninth chord voicings given there. Be sure to look over all of the dominant and minor types very carefully, since they are used extensively in the blues and related music. You'll find they can be very useful in your rhythm playing and they will give you extra notes to make your lead playing richer, too.

Next, move on to the EXERCISES section, and work through the examples there. Finally, try playing with ninth chords all over the fingerboard, injecting them into your favorite blues tunes or any other styles of music in which you think they might fit.

CHAPTER 7

ELEVENTH AND SUS4 CHORDS

The next possible extended chord after the ninth is the eleventh chord. We get the 11th, just like we get the ninth, from the second octave of the major scale. You will notice that the 11th is the same as the 4th degree of the scale. Generally, when the 7th and 9th are also present in a chord containing the eleventh, or the basic modality of the chord is minor, it is called an eleventh chord. If the 9th is not present, and the chord is a major or dominant chord, it is more often called a sus4 or 7sus4 chord. The sound and function of these two chords is often very much the same. This is why they are all discussed here in the same chapter.

At one time, there was a greater difference between the function of a sus4 chord and the function of an eleventh chord. Common practice dictated that the 4th in a sus chord was in fact a *suspension*—a *non-chord tone* or note suspended above a member of the chord which quickly resolve down to that chord member. The *suspended 4th* normally resolved down to the 3rd of the chord, which was most often major. You can still hear this treatment of the sus chords in popular music today, but it is not a hard-and-fast rule like it was in the past. Now, you can leave the suspension unresolved without offending any-one's ears. It can be a complete chord at rest in itself.

Now let's look at each of these chords individually. We'll start with the simpler sus4 and 7sus4 chords.

Sus4 and 7sus4 Chords

Building From Scales

As mentioned above, sus4 chords are a type of suspended chord. ("Sus" is short for "suspended.") In this case, the note suspended is the 4th. The way this chord is derived is by taking a triad or a seventh chord (in which case it would be called a 7sus4 chord) and *suspending the 3rd of that chord up to the next scale step* (the 4th). Since we have suspended the 3rd, the chord won't contain it; the 4th, in essence, replaces the 3rd.

If you've learned your triads and seventh chords well, you should have no trouble at all forming sus chords. If you are still a little unsure of triads and seventh chords, working on the sus4 chords will actually help you to learn them, since you need to visualize the chord before you alter it. The illustration below shows both sus4 and 7sus4 chords.

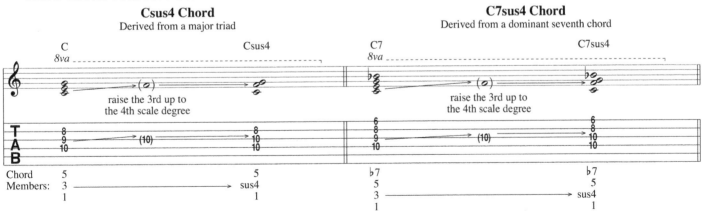

In the first example, we took a major triad and raised the 3rd up to the next step in the scale, creating a sus4 chord. In the second example, we raised the 3rd of a dominant seventh chord, resulting in a 7sus4 chord.

The Intervallic View

Building the sus4 chord with intervals is a simple matter. Starting with a triad, the bottom interval is expanded from a 3rd (in the following example, a major 3rd) to a *perfect 4th*. On top of that we place a major 2nd to get the 5th of the chord. For the 7sus4, we start with a sus4 chord and add a minor 3rd on top to get the 7th of the chord. The outside intervals remain unchanged. Here's what the two chords look like intervallically:

Intervallic View

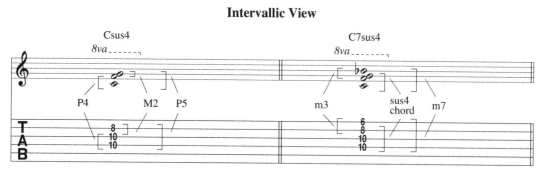

You can see you need to know the original chord before you can alter any of the notes in it. In Chapter 9 we will look at more altered chords.

Eleventh Chords

As with ninth chords, eleventh chords all contain a seventh chord within them. They function the same as, and can be used instead of, the type of seventh chord they contain (major seventh, minor seventh, or dominant seventh). The main difference between dominant eleventh chords and 7sus4 chords is the presence of the 9th. Usually the 3rd is omitted to avoid a clash with the ♮11th.

In most blues-based music, only the dominant type of eleventh chord is used, but we will look at minor eleventh chords as well, as they can also be used in this style. Major eleventh chords contain a ♯11th and will be discussed in the chapter on altered chords.

Dominant Eleventh Chords

Building From Scales

Dominant eleventh chords, as you can surmise, are derived from the major scale, using a flatted 7th degree (♭7). We add the ninth to a dominant seventh chord and place the eleventh on top to create a dominant eleventh. As stated previously, the 3rd is usually omitted, though we show it as part of the chord here. Here is how we derive the chord using a two-octave C major scale:

C Dominant Eleventh Chord

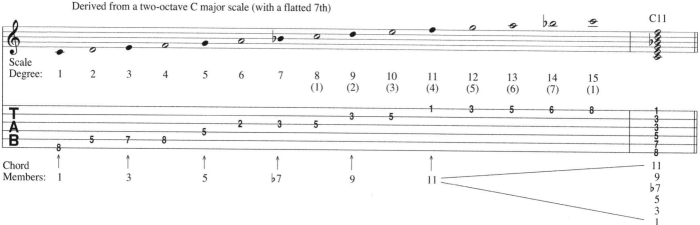

The Intervallic View

The intervals of the dominant eleventh chord stack up much in the way you would expect, starting with a dominant seventh chord (major 3rd, minor 3rd, and minor 3rd, from the bottom up.) On top of the seventh chord we add the interval of a major 3rd to get the 9th, and finally we stack a minor 3rd on top of all this to get the 11th of the chord.

If you look at the top three notes of the chord—♭7, 9, and 11—you can see that *they form a major triad using the ♭7th as the root.* A C11 chord, for example, looks like a B♭ major chord on top of a C major chord. This can be a very helpful way of looking at chords.

Here is how the intervals stack up.

C Dominant Eleventh Chord

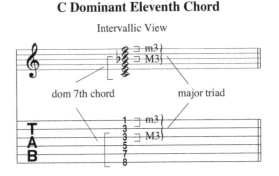

Dominant eleventh chords are used in jazz-style blues and, most extensively, in R&B tunes. They are used almost exclusively as a V chord—particularly at the end of a verse or song section. The 11th adds a brightness and a tension to the chord.

Minor Eleventh Chords

Building From Scales

To make a minor eleventh, we use the natural minor scale, starting with a minor seventh chord. The 9th and 11th are placed on top, just as with the dominant elevenths. Again, we use a two-octave scale.

C Minor Eleventh Chord

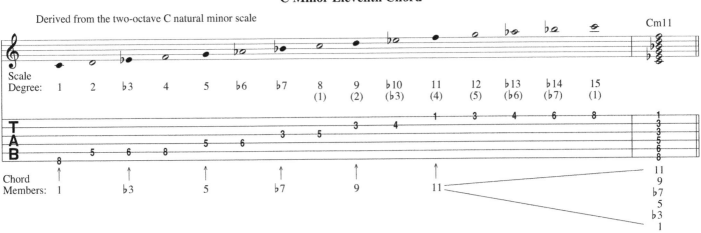

The notes are the same as those in the dominant eleventh chord except for the 3rd, which is flatted and *not* omitted. However, the 9th *can* be omitted in a minor eleventh chord. You could call the resulting chord a minor 7sus4, but we will stick with the minor eleventh label.

The Intervallic View

The intervals stack up as you would expect. On top of a minor seventh chord (minor 3rd, major 3rd, and minor 3rd) we put a major 3rd to get the 9th of the chord, and a minor 3rd to get the 11th. As with the dominant eleventh chord, you end up with a major triad on top of another chord, but this time, the bottom chord is a minor triad. With a C11 chord, for example, you would have a B♭ triad on top of a C minor triad. Here's how that looks:

C Minor Eleventh Chord

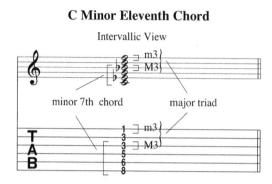

Minor eleventh chords are used primarily in jazz-style blues as well as in R&B styles, but they can be very effective in a minor blues tune if you use them *very sparingly* (maybe once in the twelve-bar cycle). They can also be used to give you a melody note if you want the 4th degree of the scale in the melody over a minor seventh or minor ninth chord.

CHAPTER 8
THIRTEENTH CHORDS

After the eleventh chord, the final possible extended chord is the thirteenth. We can't extend a chord any further because, with the thirteenth, we've used up all seven notes of the key. (The next 3rd up would be the root, two octaves up from where we started.) The full thirteenth chord contains a root, 3rd, 5th, ♭7th, 9th, and even an 11th, on top of which we stack the 13th. Every thirteenth chord contains a seventh chord, as with the other extended chords. The major seventh chord is not used to build a thirteenth chord, however, because the 13th of the chord is the same note as the 6th, which would clash with the natural 7th. We therefore only construct dominant and minor thirteenth chords.

Dominant Thirteenth Chords

Building From Scales

The 13th tone comes from the second octave of the two-octave scale used to construct chords. It is the same as the 6th degree of the scale (in the first octave) and is also the same note as the 6th of a sixth chord. It is derived just as other chord extensions are. The following diagram illustrates, using the C major scale:

C Dominant Thirteenth Chord

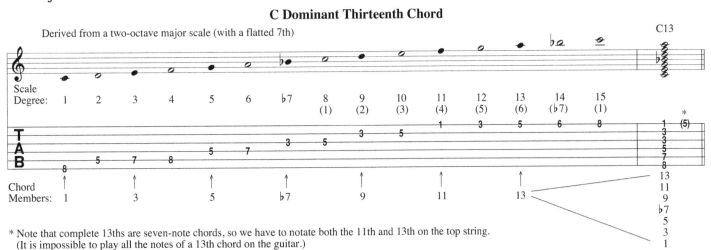

* Note that complete 13ths are seven-note chords, so we have to notate both the 11th and 13th on the top string.
  (It is impossible to play all the notes of a 13th chord on the guitar.)

As we saw, the 13th is the same note as the 6th. This can cause confusion as to what a chord actually is —a thirteenth chord or a sixth chord—and it can cause problems in choosing what notes to omit in your voicings. Just remember this: *The thirteenth chord must contain the ♭7th.* If the 7th is not there, it's not a thirteenth chord. Without the ♭7th, it's a sixth chord of some type. So you can probably guess what notes are essential in a thirteenth chord, based on the previous chapters. They are the 3rd, 7th, and 13th. That's all!

When voicing a thirteenth chord, it is important to place the 7th below the 13th to get a good sound. You can include the 9th for a stronger sense of the extension and for richer harmony, but it's not absolutely essential. You may also include the 11th in your voicing—often in place of the 3rd—for a very thick and full sound. You create quite a bit more tension with that voicing though, so you should use it sparingly.

Since the full thirteenth chord with the 11th included is a seven-note chord, and the guitar has only six strings, you can't play it. You must omit at least one note of the full chord. In practice, the 11th is most often omitted.

Many voicings contain the root on the bottom with a larger space between the lower notes than between the upper notes. When you have a chord as rich and full as a thirteenth chord, it's best to either construct them that way or to use smaller, incomplete three- or four-note chords.

The Intervallic View

The intervals of the dominant thirteenth chord are straightforward, as you should be able to guess by now. Starting with a dominant seventh chord, a major 3rd is added to get the 9th. The eleventh is a minor 3rd above, and the top interval is a major 3rd, giving you the 13th of the chord.

You can find smaller chords within the thirteenth chord structure, just as we did with the eleventh chords. You can look at it as a dominant ninth chord with a minor triad built on top (on the 9th). In the case of a C13 chord, you would have a C9 chord with a D minor triad on top of it. Here it is:

C Dominant Thirteenth Chord

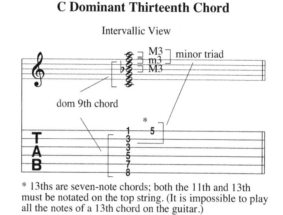

Intervallic View

* 13ths are seven-note chords; both the 11th and 13th must be notated on the top string. (It is impossible to play all the notes of a 13th chord on the guitar.)

Dominant thirteenth chords are rich and full. They add a lot of color to your harmony, and may be interchanged with dominant ninths, sixth chords, and even dominant seventh chords. However, they don't mix well with plain triads. The difference in fullness is too great. They may be used wherever dominant chords are called for, as long as you don't clash with the melody.

Dominant thirteenth chords are also used a great deal in jazz-style blues and, to a lesser extent, in some of the more "mature," jazz-like R&B styles.

Minor Thirteenth Chords

Minor thirteenth chords contain a ♮13th, which creates a problem when trying to build one from a minor scale, as we've constructed the rest of our minor chords. We could derive a minor thirteenth chord from the natural minor scale, but we'd have to alter the 13th (the 6th of the scale) to make it a ♮13th (since the 6th is flatted in a minor key). The easiest way to make a minor thirteenth chord is to take a dominant thirteenth chord and make it minor by flatting the 3rd. This is how we'll do it.

Another way to derive a minor thirteenth chord is to take a minor seventh or minor ninth chord and add the 13th to it. Remember to make it a ♮13th (found two frets above the 5th of the chord). Please note that minor thirteenth chords should contain the 9th to get the best sound. All of the examples given in the CHORDS section contain the 9th.

Here's a C minor thirteenth chord derived from a C dominant thirteenth:

C Minor Thirteenth Chord
Derived from a C13 chord

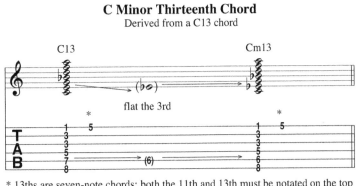

* 13ths are seven-note chords; both the 11th and 13th must be notated on the top string. (It is impossible to play all the notes of a 13th chord on the guitar.)

Minor thirteenth chords are used to some extent in jazz-style blues. You don't hear them very much, but they can also be used in rock and in some minor blues tunes.

Find minor thirteenths in the CHORDS section. You'll see that because of their size and complexity there are not many voicings available on the guitar.

CHAPTER 9

ALTERED CHORDS

The chords we have looked at so far represent the totality of *chord types* available in the tertian harmony system we are using. There are no extensions beyond the 13th of the chord. However, we can *alter* some of the members, or notes, of those chords to get some very different sounding chords. Chord members are altered by *sharping*, or raising, a note by one half step or by *flatting*, or lowering, a note one half step. Remember a half step equals one fret on the guitar.

The notes most commonly altered in blues-based music are the 5th and 9th of chords. Not all chord types commonly contain altered notes. Most often, dominant chords will support the altering of all of the above mentioned notes. Minor chords will also support some altered notes. There is only one type of major seventh chord with altered notes given here, though more are possible.

Usually only one note in a chord will be sharped or flatted, but you can have a chord with both the 5th and 9th altered (e.g., A7♯5♭9 or Cm7♭5♭9). We'll look at those chords a bit later.

The 11th can also be sharped (though not flatted—that would make it the enharmonic equivalent of a 3rd), but ♯11 chords are not generally used in blues-based music. However, we'll look at how to build them because they are used in jazz. Also, the 13th can be flatted; but in practice, the 5th of the chord is usually omitted, making it indistinguishable from a 7♯5 chord, which we'll see in this chapter.

Since we are only going to alter a note or two of the chords we've already looked at, we won't construct them again. We'll only look at how we change a note within a chord to create an altered chord.

Seven ♭5 Chords (7♭5)

We can flat the 5th of either a minor seventh or a dominant seventh chord. The sound we end up with is a much "darker" one. The minor 7♭5 chord is sometimes called a *half-diminished* chord, because it is made up of a diminished triad with a ♭7th on top. It's only half-diminished because the 7th is not doubly flatted (♭♭7) as in a fully diminished chord, and so it does not repeat every three frets as a fully diminished seventh chord does. The following diagram illustrates how both the dominant 7♭5 and minor 7♭5 chords are formed from unaltered chords.

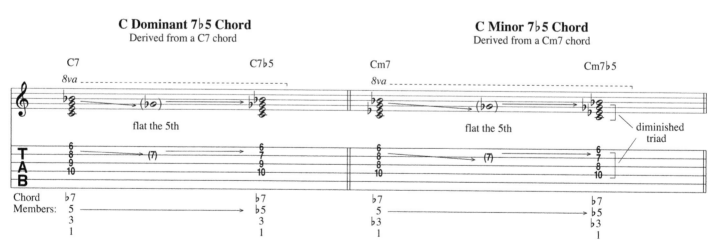

Minor 7♭5 chords are often used in minor blues for the ii or the v chords. They are also used in jazz-style blues as well as in some R&B tunes. (Check out the music of Cornell Dupree for some uses.) The dominant 7♭5 chord is used as a V chord in some minor blues tunes and jazz-style blues. You can also add the 9th or 13th of the chord to create a 9♭5 or a 13♭5. Adding the 11th wouldn't work because the ♭5 is too close in pitch and would create a tension other chord members couldn't smooth out.

Seven ♯5 Chords (7♯5)

The 7♯5 chord is always a dominant type of chord. As with the 7♭5 chords above, the 5th degree of the chord is altered, only this time we *raise it one half step*. The resulting chord is also called an *augmented seventh* chord. It is made up of an augmented triad with a ♭7th on top. See the example below.

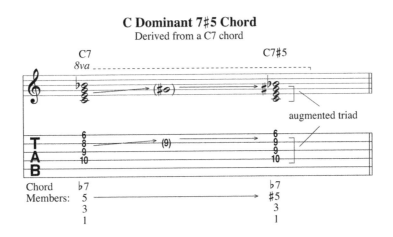

C Dominant 7♯5 Chord
Derived from a C7 chord

Again, you can add the 9th to create a 9♯5 chord, just as you could with the 7♭5 chords. These chords are used almost exclusively as V chords, where you want a lot of tension and "forward motion" to the I. They are used to a great extent in jazz-style blues.

Sharp 9 and Flat 9 Chords (7♯9, 7♭9)

These chords are more commonly referred to as 7♯9 and 7♭9 chords, to avoid any confusion. (We only alter *dominant* ninth chords—not the major or minor varieties.)

Again, it is very simple to alter the 9ths, using ninth chord voicings you have already learned. For a ♭9 chord, lower the 9th one half step. For a ♯9 chord, raise the 9th by one half step. The following diagram illustrates:

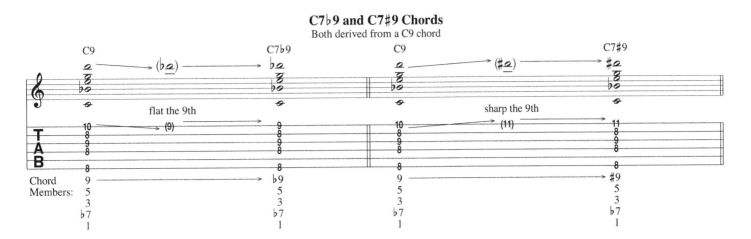

C7♭9 and C7♯9 Chords
Both derived from a C9 chord

♯9 and ♭9 chords are used quite a bit in blues and blues-based music. ♯9 chords can be used for the I or the V chords, or for both in the same tune. They don't work particularly well for the IV chord, because the raised 9th clashes in the key. (It's the ♯5th degree of the scale.) ♭9 chords can be used for the V chord, but again, the flatted 9th in a IV chord would clash.

If you use a V9 chord in a minor blues tune, it should always be altered—either sharped or flatted. They work quite well played one after the other (e.g., E7♯9 to E7♭9, resolving to the i chord, A minor). We'll look at some examples in the EXERCISES section.

You can use a ♯5 or a ♭5 along with the altered 9ths to create ♭9♭5, ♭9♯5, ♯9♯5, and ♯9♭5 chords. We'll look at examples of all of these in the CHORDS section.

When you alter any of the above mentioned notes, as we did with the ♭5, ♯5, ♭9, and ♯9 chords, you are not changing the function of the chord. Neither are you changing it's *modality* (minor or major). But you are significantly changing its sound and the "feel" it produces. As a country friend of mine puts it, you're giving it that "Big City" sound.

Altered chords also have a more dissonant sound, often creating an unsettling feeling. They should be used with care and you should pay close attention to how well they fit in a given tune. The altered notes can clash with melody notes. If in the vocals, for example, the melody contains a note in its unaltered form against your altered chord (e.g., you play a 7♯5 chord and the melody contains an unaltered, ♮5), there will be a clash.

If you're playing with a group, you may need to work out the chord choices in advance with the other players. If you play an A7♯9 chord while a keyboard player plays a straight unaltered A9 chord, there could be a clash. Everybody needs to alter the same notes in the same way for it to work. However, if the keyboard player plays a plain A7, and you choose to play an A7♯9 or an A7♭9, there will be no clash because only you play the 9th.

Sharp 11 Chords

Major ♯11

Major ♯11 chords contain a major seventh chord and include a raised or sharped 11th. The 3rd must be present in the voicing, and some patterns on the guitar allow you to include the 9th. The root can be omitted, and the 5th should be, since it is only one half step away from the ♯11 (the same note as a ♯4). We can derive a major ♯11 chord using a major seventh chord. The resulting chord will have the essential notes, which are the 1, 3, ♮7, and ♯11, and the non-essential 9th. Here's how it looks.

C Major 7♯11 Chord
Derived from a Cmaj7 chord

These chords, as beautiful as they sound, must be used very carefully and sparingly. They make a very good ending chord for a tune with a lot of major seventh and major ninth chords in it. They also make a nice "psychedelic" type of chord. They can be found in jazz tunes, especially as a final chord.

Dominant ♯11

You may also sharp the 11th of a dominant chord (7♯11), creating a dissonant chord that really needs to resolve properly (usually from a V7♯11 to a I or Imaj7). We can derive this chord simply by taking an eleventh chord and sharping the 11th. The following diagram demonstrates this.

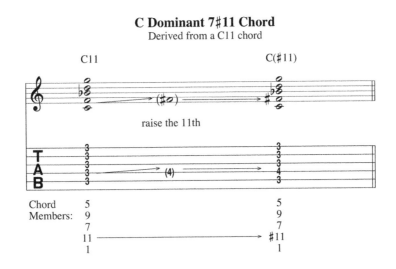

Dominant 7♯11 chords are not used a great deal except in jazz-style blues. If you would like to jazz up your chords, you can try them in your blues playing and see how they work for you.

Extended Chords Containing Altered Notes

You can add extensions to the above altered chords. Some common examples are:

- 9♭5 (7♭5 chord with a ♮9th added)
- 9♯5 (7♯5 chord with a ♮9th added)
- 7♯5♭9 (a 7♯5 chord with a ♭9 added)
- 7♯5♯9 (a 7♯5 chord with a ♯9 added)
- 13♭9 (a ♭9 chord with the 13th added)

Not every alteration or extension will work all the time. At times, some will sound too dissonant. This is really a matter of personal taste, of course. Try to experiment by altering notes in chords that you already know, and see how you like their "altered" sound.

Combined Altered Notes in a Chord

As mentioned earlier, you may alter more than one note in a chord. Some of the more common examples are $7\flat5\flat9$, $7\sharp5\flat9$, and $7\sharp5\sharp9$.

You already know from the earlier sections of this chapter how to alter the above-mentioned notes of the chords; you simply alter two notes instead of one, or you add extensions to the chord you have altered. In the CHORDS section we will look at only a few voicings of the chords listed here, but you can experiment with any of the chords you have learned. You may end up with a great tune or style as a result.

Now move on to the CHORDS section and look up the altered chords. Learn them in the same fashion you learned the other chords. A particularly effective method of learning them is to take a seventh chord (minor or dominant) and alter the 5th (both sharp and flat). Then do the same with all of the rest of the voicings for the seventh chord. Then add extensions to it (9ths, 11ths, and 13ths). Then do the same with dominant ninth chords. The more you work through the chords, the better you will learn how they work and the better you will know the fingerboard.

After you have done some of this work, look at the altered chords part of the EXERCISES section.

CHAPTER 10
OTHER CHORDS

We have looked at all of the basic chord types, from triads through thirteenth chords, including alterations of those basic types. Now we will complete our survey of chords by looking at a few other chord types.

Not all chords in the tertian harmony system follow the "every other scale degree" construction system we have been using (i.e. 1-3-5-7-9-11-13). We have already seen that sixth chords, for example, are built a little differently, although we still use the notes of the scale to build them. Similarly, there are several more chord types that are constructed with non-3rd chord tones added to the basic triads. They are for the most part used only for special effects or sounds, but they can be found in blues-based music.

Add9 Chords

Add9 chords are made up of a major or minor triad with the 9th added on to it. The 9th is the same note as the second degree of the major or minor scale. *There is no 7th included in an add9 chord.* Because of the absence of the 7th, add9 chords don't qualify as actual ninth chords and don't function as dominant chords either. They do contain a complete triad, with no notes omitted. The following diagram shows how add9 chords are constructed.

C Major and Minor Add9 Chords

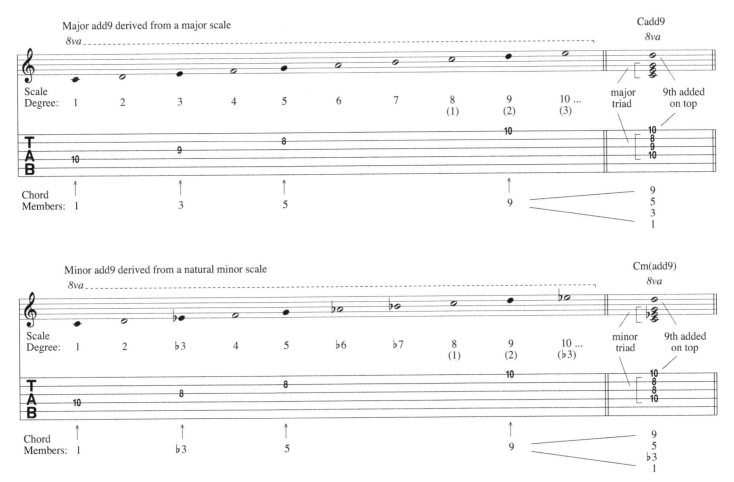

Add9 chords are most often used in rock and R&B styles. When the 9th is added on top of a chord, it creates a bright and "shimmering" sound—particularly with the major add9, which is very pretty. When the 9th is added in the middle notes of a chord, dissonance and tension are created. Add9 chords are often used before and/or after a straight triad, as we will see in the exercises which follow.

You can hear add9 chords in the prettier and spacier tunes of Jimi Hendrix and Stevie Ray Vaughan, as well as in the music of Curtis Mayfield, who pioneered their use. I can think of no straight, twelve-bar blues tune where they are used. However, they can be used anywhere a major or minor chord is indicated.

Six/Nine Chords (6/9)

Six/nine chords are very beautiful chords, made up of a major or minor sixth chord with the 9th added. Again, there is no 7th present in the chord. Unlike the add9 chords, the root or 5th of the chord may be omitted in your voicings without changing the essence of the chord. You will notice that the 9th is always placed *above* the 6th of the chord. Here's how they are constructed.

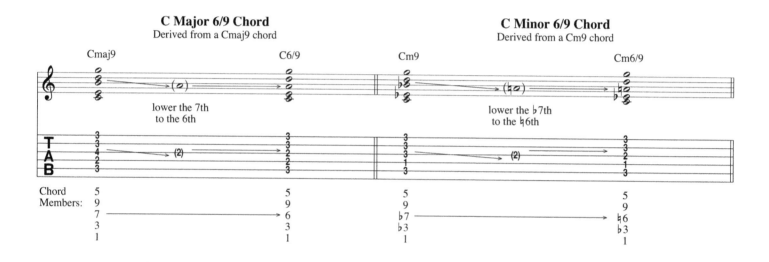

Six/nine chords are used primarily in jazz-style blues and some R&B tunes. They can be used as a I or a IV chord in jazz-style blues tunes, but most often they are used as the "ending" or final I chord in a tune, making it clear "the tune is over."

Minor-Major Seventh Chords [Min(Maj 7)]

Minor-major seventh chords are very interesting and beautiful, if rarely used, chords. They are constructed by placing a ♮7 on top of a minor triad, which means the outer interval between the root and the 7th of the chord is a major 7th. You end up with a minor chord that has a major 7th, thus the term minor-major seventh. Looking at it another way, you take a minor seventh chord and *raise the 7th one half step*. The resulting chord is unique sounding. Its construction is illustrated here.

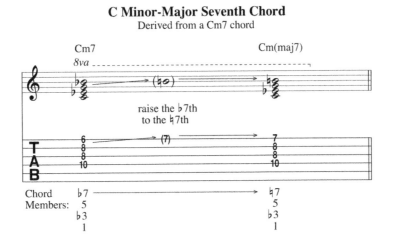

C Minor-Major Seventh Chord
Derived from a Cm7 chord

Minor-major seventh chords are used in the blues, in jazz-style blues, and in some R&B tunes. Their use is rare but effective. Primarily, they are used in passing; they are not meant to stand alone but rather to move from one chord to the minor ♮7 and then to another chord. They are a little too dissonant to be sounded for any length of time. Most commonly, they follow a straight minor chord and move to a minor seventh chord, all within the same root. Often the progression moves on to a minor sixth chord, again with the same root. The result is a chromatic line that moves by half steps from the root through the ♮7 and the ♭7 to the 6th. (We'll see this in detail in the pages of the EXERCISES section.)

Look at the voicings given in the CHORDS section. There are not a lot given because there are not a lot of usable voicings for these unusual chords. Then work through the examples in the EXERCISES section.

This section contains chord voicings that are useful for blues-based music. There are, as stated earlier, more voicings possible than the ones which follow, including some so difficult to finger that they are impractical for everyday playing. I encourage you to look for other voicings and decide for yourself if they are useful to you or not.

The voicings follow the same order as in the THEORY section (triads, then seventh chords, and so on).

TRIADS

We'll start by looking at the smallest and simplest voicings possible—triads with no doubled notes (three-note chords) played on consecutive strings. Then we'll look at voicings using non-consecutive strings, skipping and muting a string or two in the middle, and finally, we'll try some larger voicings, which make use of four or more consecutive strings.

Closed Voicings

Using strings 3, 2, and 1:

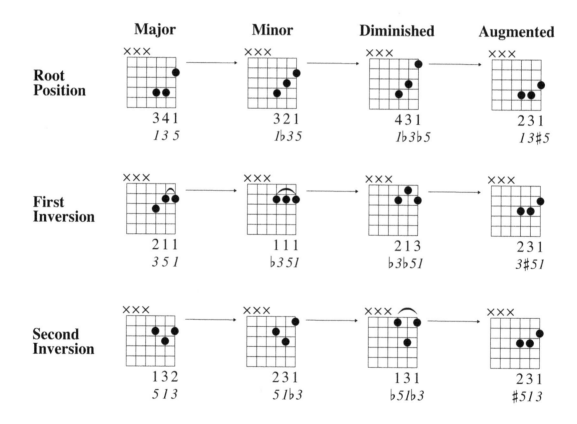

Using strings 4, 3, and 2:

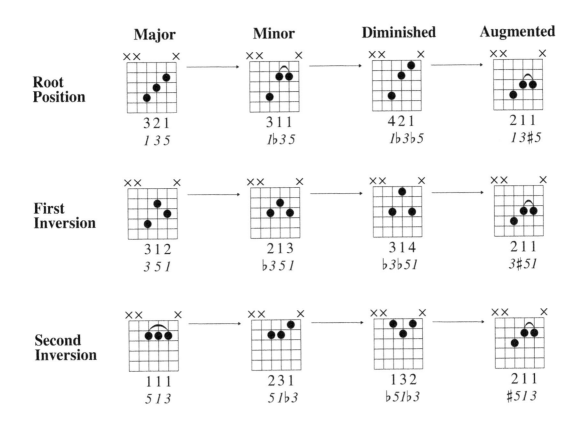

Using strings 5, 4, and 3:

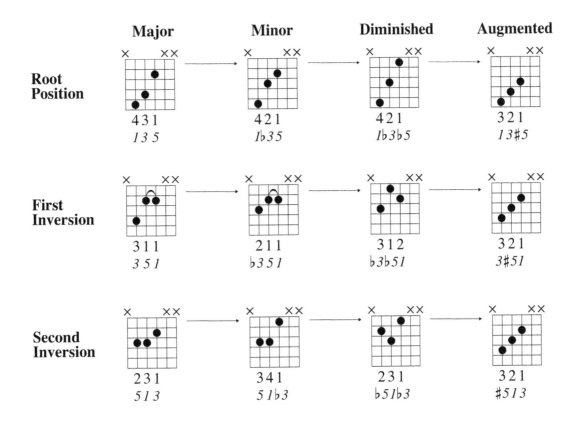

Using strings 6, 5, and 4:

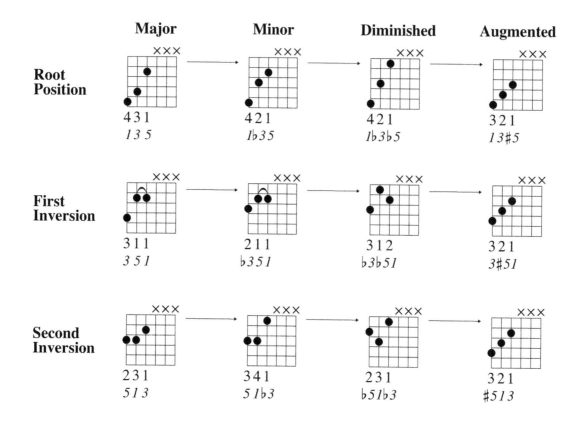

Open Voicings

Here are some open voicings. They're nice and clean sounding with the notes spread further apart. You'll find they're good for situations where other instruments are also playing chords.

Using strings 4 through 1:

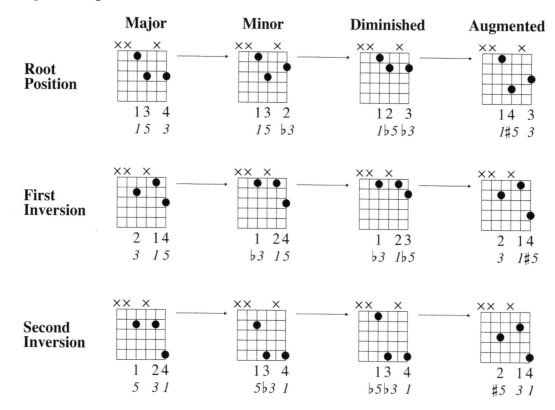

Using strings 5 through 2:

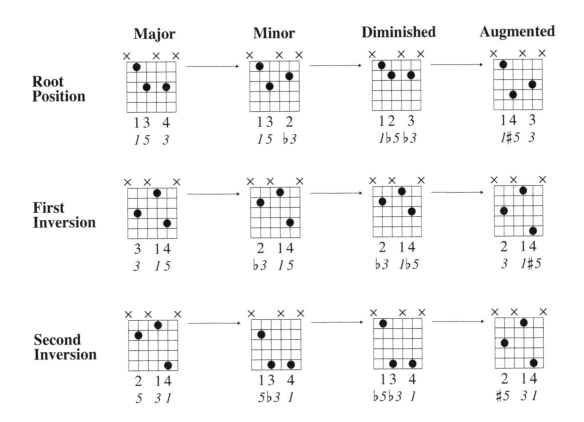

Using strings 6 through 3:

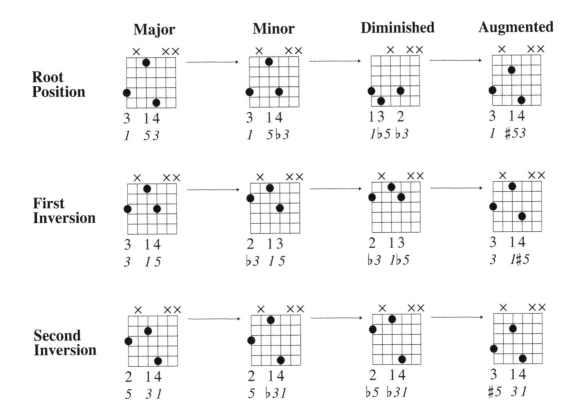

Larger Voicings: Major and Minor Forms

The preceding chords can be combined to make larger voicings, making use of doubling as described in Chapter 2. The following chord forms are not all the larger forms you can use, but they are forms I've found useful in playing blues and blues-based music.

You'll notice we don't include diminished or augmented chords here. This is because we don't often double notes in diminished triads; we'll look at some doubling in augmented chords next. Notice some voicings work well for major triads but not for minor, and vice versa.

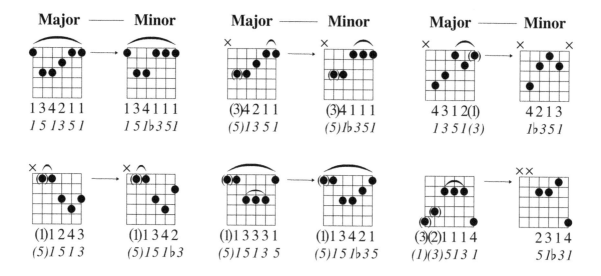

Major —— Minor	Major —— Minor	Major —— Minor
1 3 4 2 1 1 1 3 4 1 1 1	(3)4 2 1 1 (3)4 1 1 1	4 3 1 2(1) 4 2 1 3
1 5 1 3 5 1 *1 5 1♭3 5 1*	*(5)1 3 5 1* *(5)1♭3 5 1*	*1 3 5 1(3)* *1♭3 5 1*
(1)1 2 4 3 (1)1 3 4 2	(1)1 3 3 3 1 (1)1 3 4 2 1	(3)(2)1 1 1 4 2 3 1 4
(5)1 5 1 3 *(5)1 5 1♭3*	*(5)1 5 1 3 5* *(5)1 5 1♭3 5*	*(1)(3)5 1 3 1* *5 1♭3 1*

Larger Voicings: Augmented Forms

Augmented chords can have doubled notes. It is generally thought the 5th of the chord, because it is "altered," should not be doubled. You'll have to use your ear to decide whether or not you agree.

As we saw in previous pages, the shapes of the inversions of augmented chords are alike, since the octave is divided evenly. This holds true even when notes are doubled. We'll limit ourselves to the doubling of only one note in the chord, and to playing the notes on consecutive strings.

On strings 6 through 3:   **On strings 5 through 2:**   **On strings 4 through 1:**

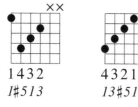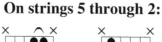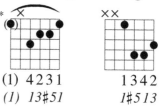

On strings 6 through 3:	On strings 5 through 2:	On strings 4 through 1:
1 4 3 2 4 3 2 1	3 2 1 1 1 4 2 3	(1) 4 2 3 1 1 3 4 2
1♯5 1 3 *1 3♯5 1*	*1 3♯5 1* *1♯5 1 3*	*(1) 1 3♯5 1* *1♯5 1 3*

*Note: The tip of the first finger
should relax and mute the 5th string.

SEVENTH CHORDS

For those who are exclusively interested in the blues, the dominant seventh and minor seventh chords are what you are looking for, and you can skip the major seventh chords for the time being. However, you should check them out later if you choose to skip them now. They are very beautiful and useful chords for other styles of music, including R&B and jazz-style blues.

Complete Closed Voicings

The first set of seventh chords given here are *complete* chords played on four consecutive strings. They are very nice voicings and can be used in any type of setting.

Using strings 4 through 1:

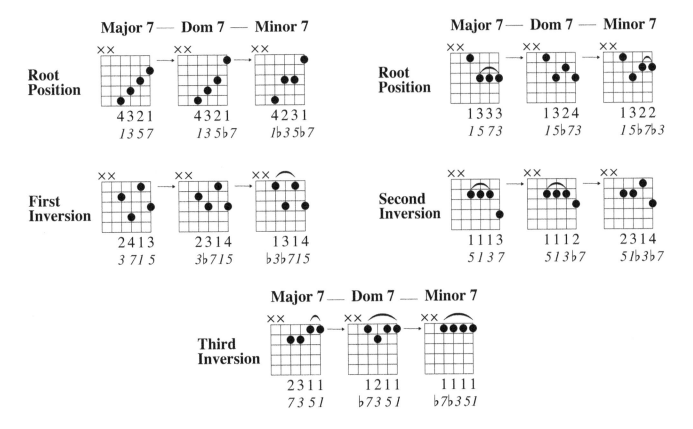

Using strings 5 through 2:

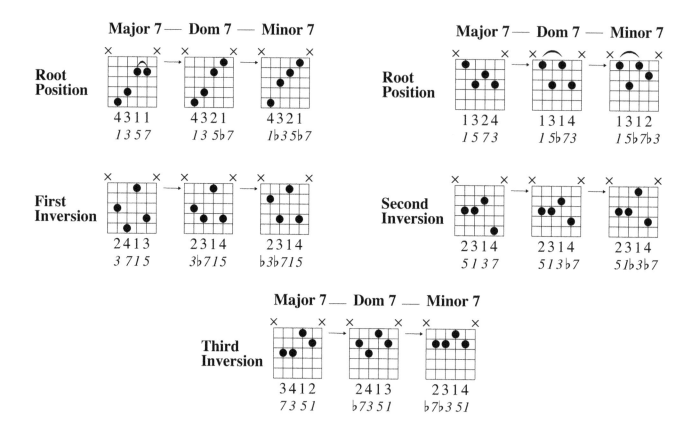

Using strings 6 through 3:

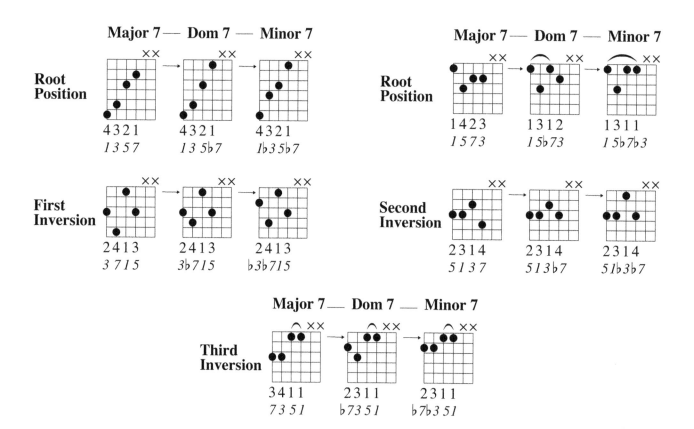

Complete Open Voicings

These next voicings are also complete seventh chords, but the notes are spread out a little. They give you a more "classical" sound because they follow the old practice of having larger intervals on the bottom of the chord and smaller intervals on top.

Using strings 6 through 2:

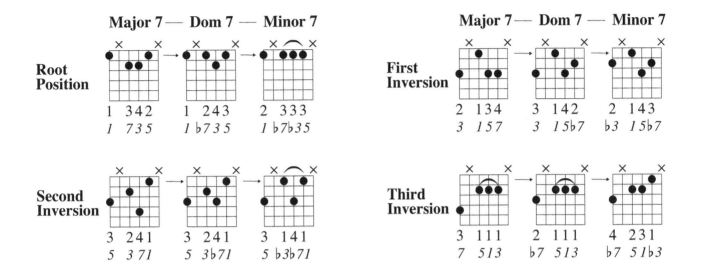

Using strings 5 through 1:

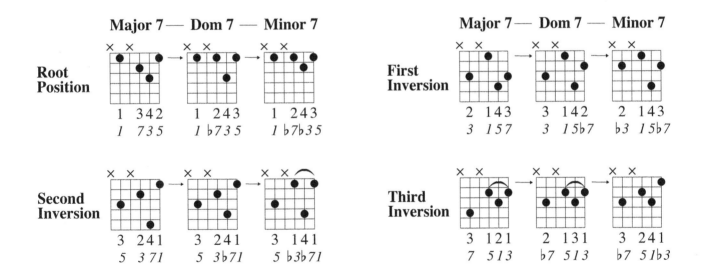

Incomplete Three-Note Forms

After you have learned the preceding voicings, try omitting the root or 5th in each of them and see how they sound. These smaller three-note chords work very well with "thick" arrangements using other chordal instruments or horns. Here are some of my favorites:

Using strings 3 through 1:

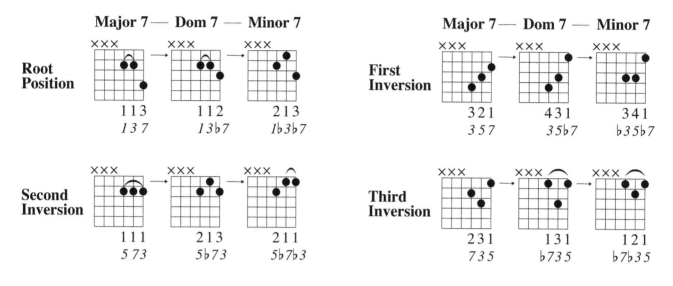

Using strings 4 through 2:

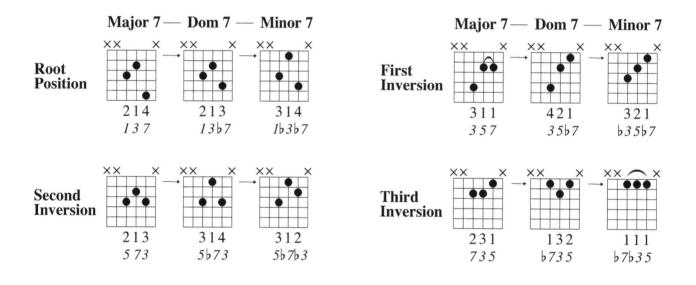

You'll usually want to have the bass or some other instrument provide the omitted notes, particularly the root. You may notice the above examples include only the upper strings; in my opinion, these voicings get a little muddy on the lower ones. Try them for yourself though to see what you think. Be sure to look for other three-note voicings because the above set is by no means exhaustive. You can use the fingerboard diagrams in the APPENDIX to help you find them. Besides finding useful chord forms, you'll learn chord construction and the layout of the fingerboard.

Larger Forms (Using Doubling)

Finally, we can build larger chord voicings by doubling some of the notes. These chords are quite lush and thick, and should be used sparingly if you're playing with another guitarist or keyboard player.

These larger forms don't always work for all three types of sevenths. Sometimes a voicing might work for a major seventh chord, but when you flat the 7th to make a dominant seventh chord, the fingering becomes difficult or impossible. In such cases, the ones which don't work are simply omitted.

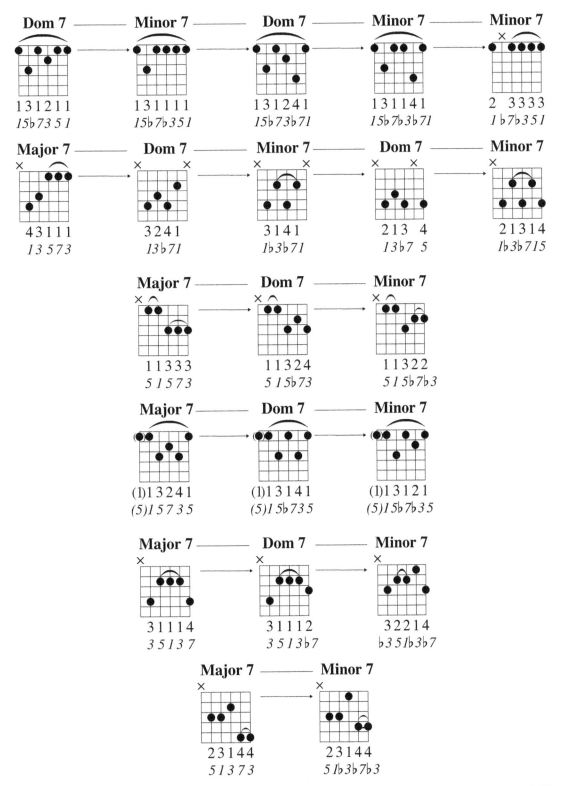

Once again, the chord voicings given above are not the only ones available on the fingerboard. You may find other forms you like the sound of, or other forms which fit your hands better than mine. I strongly encourage you to look over the whole fingerboard for more voicings in all keys.

DIMINISHED SEVENTH CHORDS

The following seven chord forms represent all of the practical voicings for diminished seventh chords. Recall from the THEORY section that they repeat every third fret and that any one of the notes in these chord forms can be the root. For that reason the chord members (1, ♭3, ♭5, ♭♭7) are not marked under the diagrams as they are under the other chords.

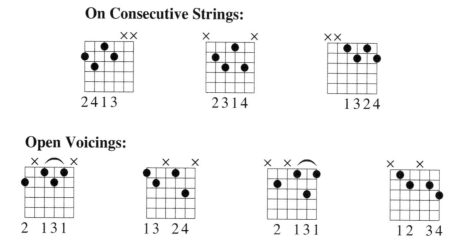

You'll find lots of interesting uses for diminished seventh chords in the EXERCISES section. Look for them in the later ninth and thirteenth chord examples as well.

SIXTH CHORDS

There are just a few sixth chord voicings I consider very useful for blues or blues-based music. They are all given here. As always, you are encouraged to find your own voicings. A full fingerboard diagram with sixth chords laid out on it can be found in the APPENDIX.

Closed Voicings

Using strings 4 through 1:

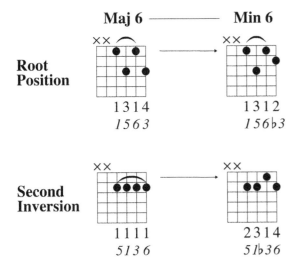

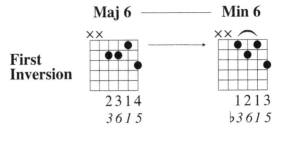

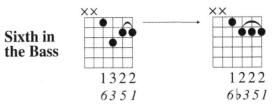

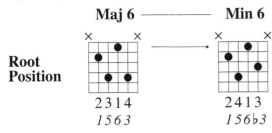

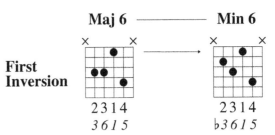

Using strings 5 through 2:

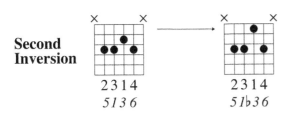

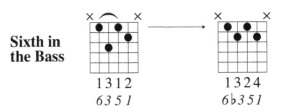

Using strings 6 through 3:

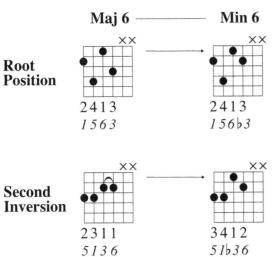

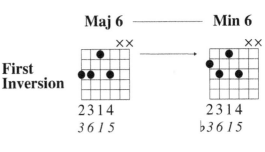

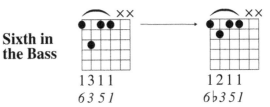

Open Voicings

Using strings 6 through 2:

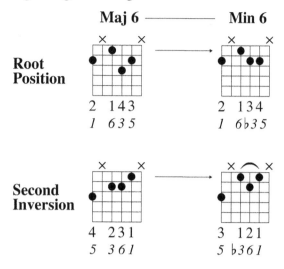

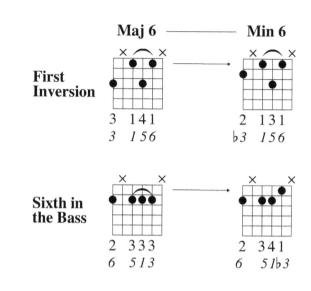

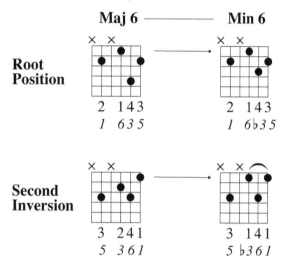

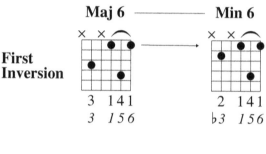

Using strings 5 through 1:

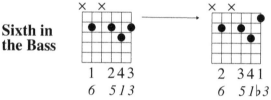

Larger Forms (Using Doubling)

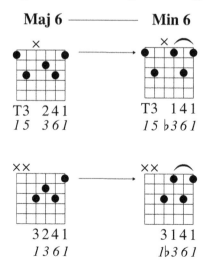

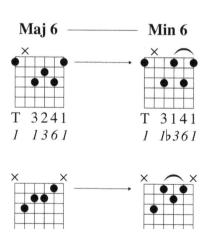

NINTH CHORDS

Closed Voicings

The chords in this first group contain all five chord members (1, 3, 5, 7, and 9). None are omitted. Some of these shapes are a bit difficult to finger as a result, which is why we often omit notes and rearrange their natural order.

Once again, if you are only interested in the blues, you may skip the major ninth chords for now. The dominant ninth chords will be of most use to you, though the minor chord ninths are useful, as well.

On strings 5 through 1:

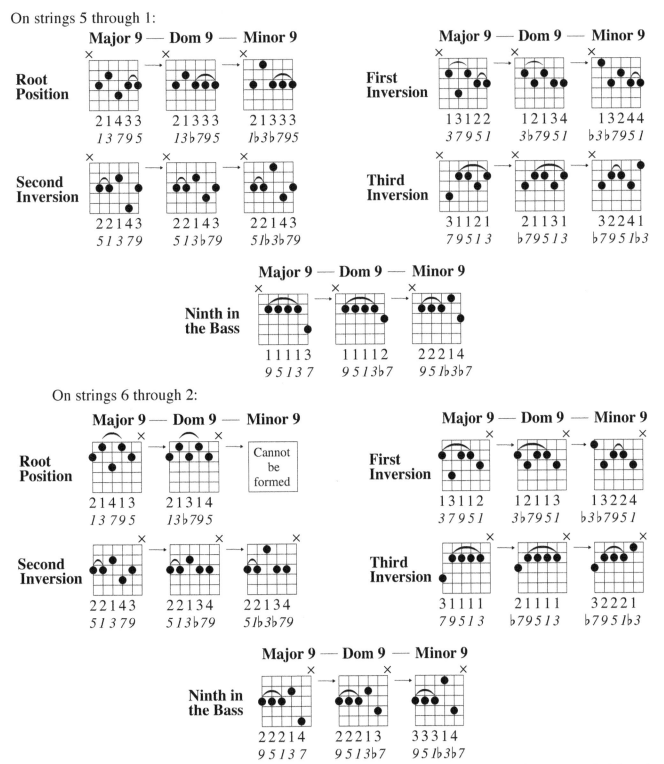

On strings 6 through 2:

Notice that in the above two groups of voicings, the only difference in the patterns is the use of either the low E (6th) string or the high E (1st) string. The rest of the notes fall in exactly the same place on the guitar for each inversion. This is because the outside strings (6th and 1st) are the same note, two octaves apart; on the same fret, they are the same chord member.

Open Voicings

Here are some complete ninth chords using open voicings:

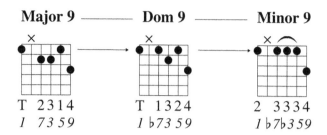

Incomplete Four-Note Forms

Most often, we use voicings which omit the root or the 5th of the chord. We can even use voicings which omit the 3rd, but we have to be careful with their use. In such instances, the 3rd should be supplied either by another instrument or by another voicing which closely follows the first. We'll look at some examples in the EXERCISES section. Work through the following voicings, paying close attention to which notes are included in the chord and where they lie.

On strings 4 through 1:

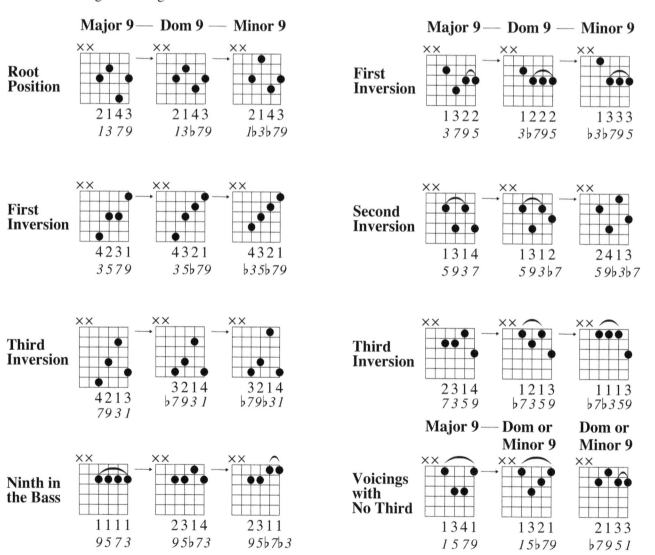

On strings 5 through 2:

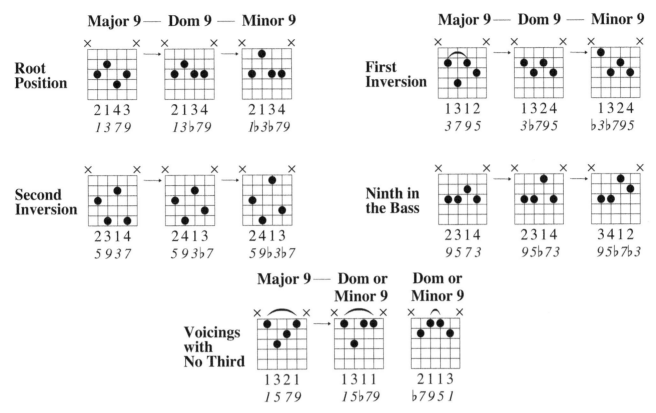

Incomplete Three-Note Forms

You can omit two notes from a ninth chord and still keep its essential character, provided you keep the 7th and 9th, of course. I'll give you a few examples below, but you should experiment with them and see which ones you like. They work nicely when you move quickly from one to the next, or even if you mix them with sevenths and thirteenths, as long as you use the same *quality* of chord (i.e., major, minor, or dominant).

Three-note chords:

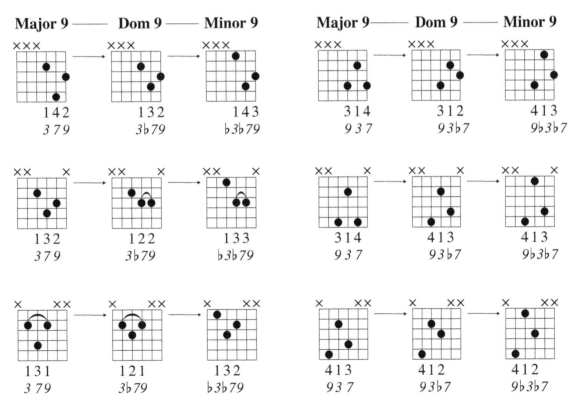

Incomplete Open Voicings

Here are some voicings that are spread out a little:

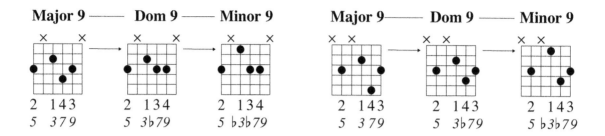

Major 9 ——— Dom 9 ——— Minor 9

2 1 4 3   2 1 3 4   2 1 3 4
5 3 7 9   5 3♭7 9   5 ♭3♭7 9

Major 9 ——— Dom 9 ——— Minor 9

2 1 4 3   2 1 4 3   2 1 4 3
5 3 7 9   5 3♭7 9   5 ♭3♭7 9

As in previous chapters, I have not given you every possible, usable voicing there is. Look over the fingerboard chart showing ninth chords in the APPENDIX, and see if you can find more. As always, it will be time well spent.

Now work on the examples in the EXERCISES section. Because there are more chords to work with, these exercises should be interesting and fun.

SUS4, 7SUS4, and ELEVENTH CHORDS

Sus4 Chords

You can take any major triad voicing and raise the 3rd one half step to the suspended 4th, making a sus4 chord. You should go through all the major triad voicings given at the beginning of this section and try this. Since it should be a fairly simple matter, I'll only include a few of the many possible voicings here so that you can see how it works. These voicings are among my favorites.

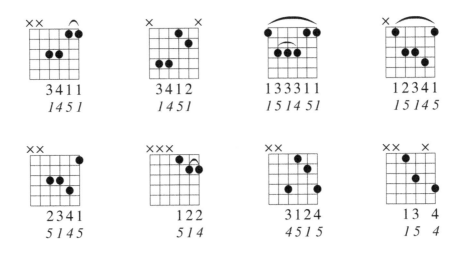

7sus4 Chords

Just as you can create sus4 chords from any of the major triad voicings, you can change a dominant seventh chord into a 7sus4 chord, again by raising the 3rd a half step to the suspended 4th. Not all the seventh chord voicings lend themselves easily to this change, but try them all and see which ones you like. As always, this type of exercise can only reinforce your knowledge of chords and of the fingerboard. Here are a few examples of some of the more useful voicings.

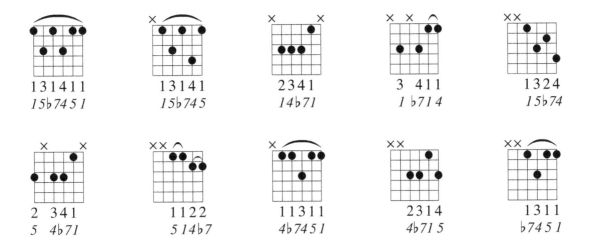

Eleventh Chords

The following eleventh chord voicings all contain the essential chord members (♭7, 9, and 11). There are other possibilities, and I strongly encourage you to find them on the fingerboard.

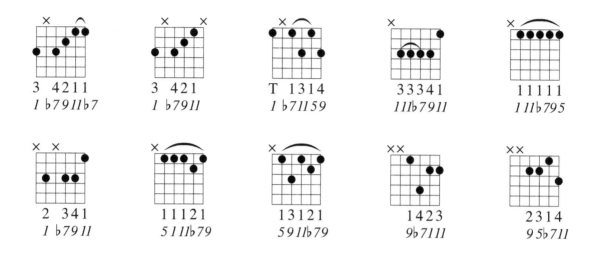

THIRTEENTH CHORDS

The voicings included here are ones I find particularly useful, or at least very interesting. As you'll see, some of these chords have an unusual sound.

Dominant Thirteenth Chords

Five- and six-note forms:

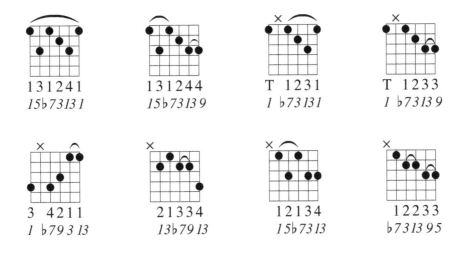

Three- and four-note forms:

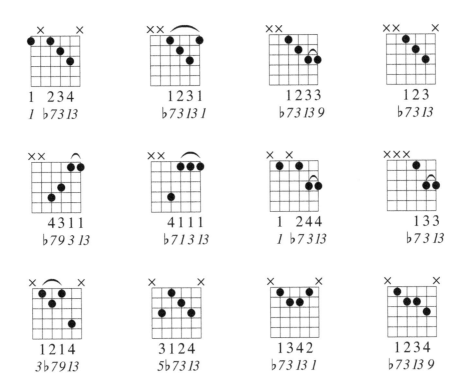

Forms containing the 11th:

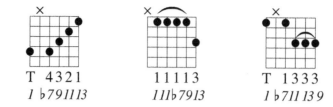

T 4 3 2 1   1 1 1 1 3   T 1 3 3 3
1 ♭7 9 11 13   *11 11 ♭7 9 13*   *1 ♭7 11 11 13 9*

Minor Thirteenth Chords

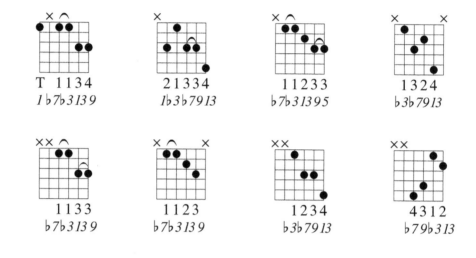

T 1 1 3 4   2 1 3 3 4   1 1 2 3 3   1 3 2 4
1 ♭7 ♭3 13 9   *1 ♭3 ♭7 9 13*   *♭7 ♭3 13 9 5*   *♭3 ♭7 9 13*

1 1 3 3   1 1 2 3   1 2 3 4   4 3 1 2
♭7 ♭3 13 9   *♭7 ♭3 13 9*   *♭3 ♭7 9 13*   *♭7 9 ♭3 13*

ALTERED CHORDS

The following voicings are quite useful for most blues styles. You may find some of them to be a bit dissonant for your own personal taste. However, I encourage you to play through them all and give them an "open ear."

Dominant 7♭5 Chords

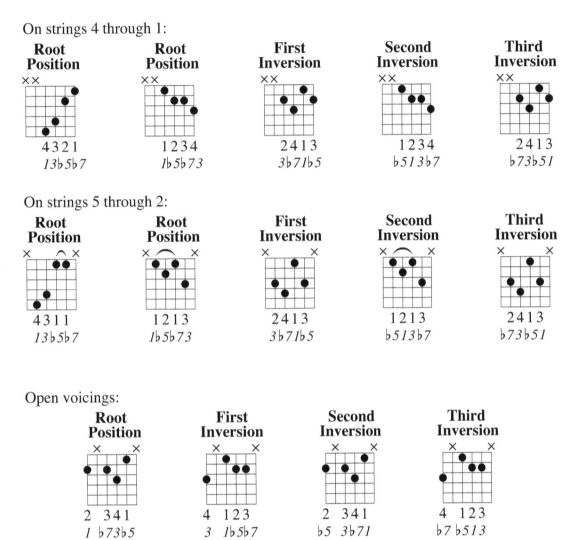

On strings 4 through 1:

Root Position	Root Position	First Inversion	Second Inversion	Third Inversion
4 3 2 1	1 2 3 4	2 4 1 3	1 2 3 4	2 4 1 3
1 3♭5♭7	1♭5♭7 3	3♭7 1♭5	♭5 1 3♭7	♭7 3♭5 1

On strings 5 through 2:

Root Position	Root Position	First Inversion	Second Inversion	Third Inversion
4 3 1 1	1 2 1 3	2 4 1 3	1 2 1 3	2 4 1 3
1 3♭5♭7	1♭5♭7 3	3♭7 1♭5	♭5 1 3♭7	♭7 3♭5 1

Open voicings:

Root Position	First Inversion	Second Inversion	Third Inversion
2 3 4 1	4 1 2 3	2 3 4 1	4 1 2 3
1 ♭7 3♭5	3 1♭5♭7	♭5 3♭7 1	♭7 ♭5 1 3

2 3 4 1	3 1 4 2	2 3 4 1	3 1 4 2
1 ♭7 3♭5	3 1♭5♭7	♭5 3♭7 1	♭7 ♭5 1 3

Minor 7♭5 Chords

On strings 4 through 1:

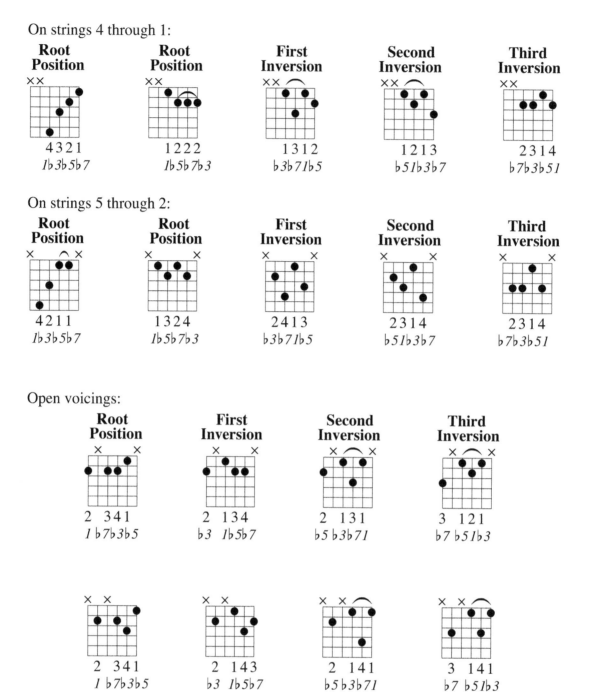

Open voicings:

66

Dominant 7♯5 (Augmented Seventh) Chords

On strings 4 through 1:

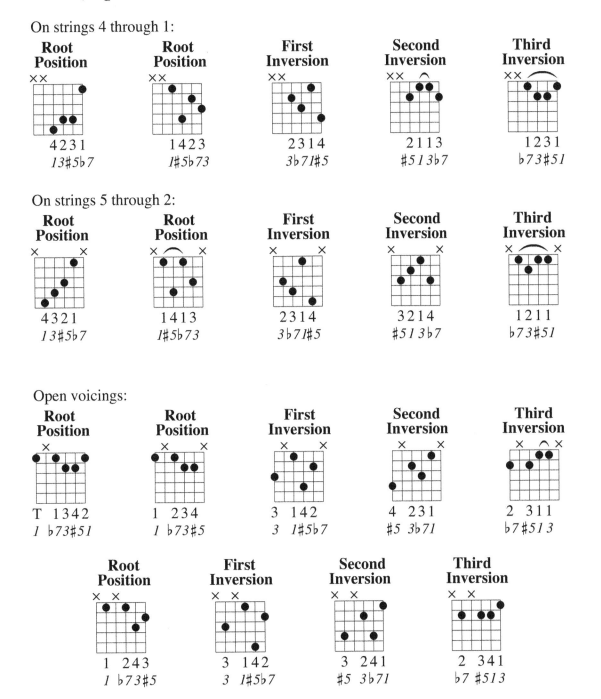

Root Position	**Root Position**	**First Inversion**	**Second Inversion**	**Third Inversion**
4 2 3 1	1 4 2 3	2 3 1 4	2 1 1 3	1 2 3 1
13♯5♭7	*1♯5♭73*	*3♭71♯5*	*♯513♭7*	*♭73♯51*

On strings 5 through 2:

Root Position	**Root Position**	**First Inversion**	**Second Inversion**	**Third Inversion**
4 3 2 1	1 4 1 3	2 3 1 4	3 2 1 4	1 2 1 1
13♯5♭7	*1♯5♭73*	*3♭71♯5*	*♯513♭7*	*♭73♯51*

Open voicings:

Root Position	**Root Position**	**First Inversion**	**Second Inversion**	**Third Inversion**
T 1 3 4 2	1 2 3 4	3 1 4 2	4 2 3 1	2 3 1 1
1 ♭73♯51	*1 ♭73♯5*	*3 1♯5♭7*	*♯5 3♭71*	*♭7♯51 3*

Root Position	**First Inversion**	**Second Inversion**	**Third Inversion**
1 2 4 3	3 1 4 2	3 2 4 1	2 3 4 1
1 ♭73♯5	*3 1♯5♭7*	*♯5 3♭71*	*♭7 ♯513*

Dominant ♯9 and ♭9 Chords

Complete altered 9th chord forms:

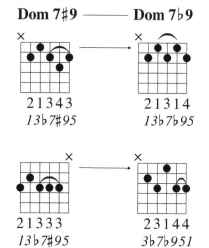

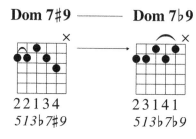

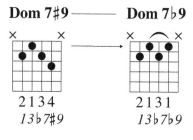

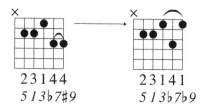

Incomplete forms:

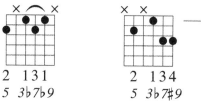

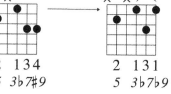

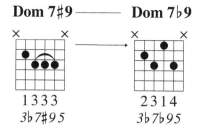

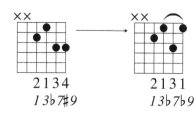

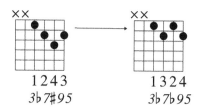

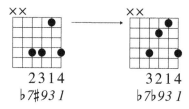

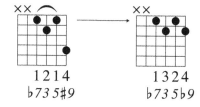

Major and Dominant 7♯11 Chords

Major 7♯11 chords:

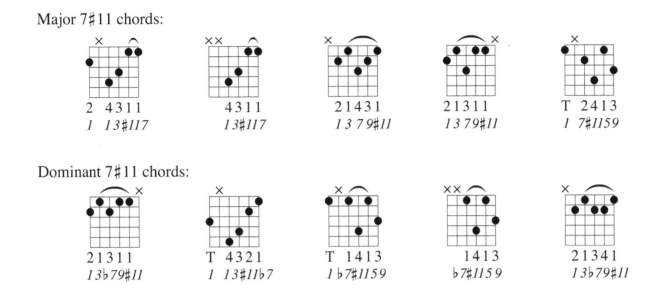

Dominant 7♯11 chords:

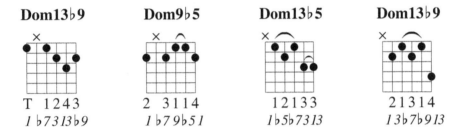

Extended Altered Chords

Following are just a few examples of the possibilities available for extended chords containing altered notes. See what you can come up with on your own.

Dom13♭9 **Dom9♭5** **Dom13♭5** **Dom13♭9**

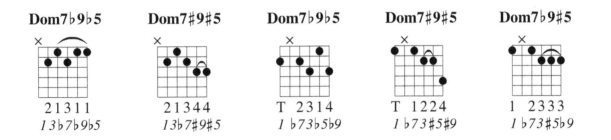

Multiple Altered Notes

Here are some examples containing more than one altered note.

Dom7♭9♭5 **Dom7♯9♯5** **Dom7♭9♭5** **Dom7♯9♯5** **Dom7♭9♯5**

Now go to the EXERCISES section to better see how the altered notes work with some examples of their use in the blues and other blues-based music.

OTHER CHORDS

Major and Minor Add9 Chords

The voicings given here are not at all exhaustive but are ones I have found to be most useful. You can take any major or minor triad voicing and add the 9th. I encourage you to do so—you may find some you like.

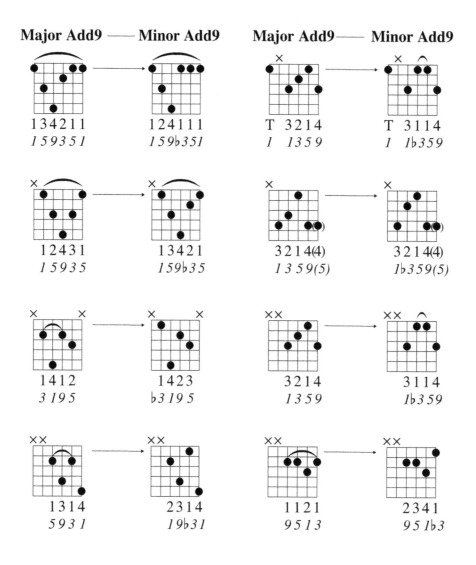

Major and Minor 6/9 Chords

As with the add9 chords, these aren't all of the forms for 6/9 chords. See if you can find some others.

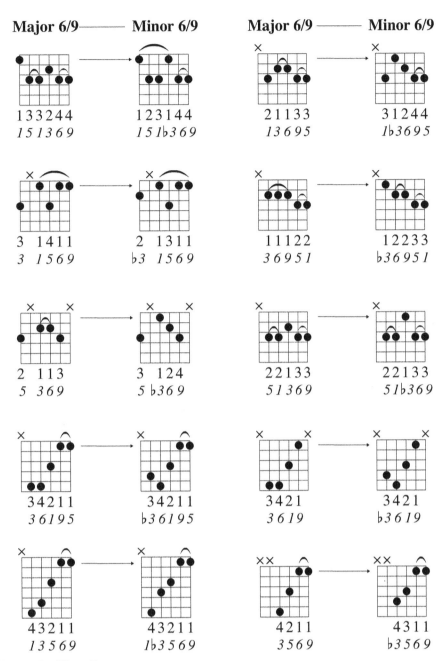

Minor-Major Seventh Chords

Here are some useful voicings. Try changing each of the minor seventh chords you know to minor-major seventh chords by raising the 7th.

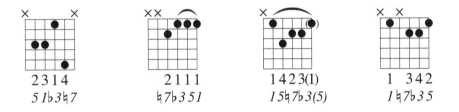

Look in the EXERCISES section for examples of the use of the above chords.

SECTION 3: EXERCISES

This section contains extensive exercises designed to teach all the forms and inversions of chords appearing in the preceding sections. It also gives examples that show how to use these chords in blues and blues-based music. These exercises are not exhaustive, and not every form is used; it is up to you to apply additional voicings to the exercises and examples given.

The exercises are given in one key with the expectation you will transpose them to *all keys*. This is very important. Only by learning them in all keys will you truly learn chords and how they lie on the fingerboard.

The exercises follow the same order as in the previous sections, with triad exercises appearing first, seventh chords next, and so on. You don't necessarily have to work completely through each set of exercises before moving on to the next set. If you find you are anxious to move on to the seventh chord exercises before you've completed the triad group, for instance, go ahead. Just remember each group of extended chords is built on simpler ones covered earlier in this section.

As you're working through the chords, the following method will help you perfect your chordal knowledge and technique.

- Review what notes are in a chord.
- Find which note is in the bass for each inversion.
- Locate that note on the guitar.

Only after you've done all of that, should you actually grab the chord on the fingerboard.

Many of the examples in this section provide a good workout through the various voicings. However, in actual playing you would seldom jump around from form to form as in the following exercises. Usually you would play voicings found near each other on the fingerboard, and you wouldn't use so many different voicings of the same chord in one tune.

One last point before we move on to the exercises. Some of the more technical exercises can become a little tedious. I have tried to keep these down to a minimum. Nonetheless, it's important to work through the various voicings in an organized manner. When you find your attention wandering—and certainly before you get glassy-eyed—stop work on that exercise and try something else. You'll find some voicings have a sound that grabs you. Go with that, and play around with those chords in particular, using them in songs you know or making up your own songs or chordal riffs with them. This can be a lot of fun.

The important thing to remember is to transpose those riffs and songs you are enjoying to all keys. It involves a fair amount of thought, but you will learn a lot by doing it.

Triads

Exercise 1 — Inversions

This exercise is intended to run through all triad inversions in every possible voicing. You are given all of the three-note voicings using consecutive strings 3 through 1 and 4 through 2 in the key of C major. It's up to you to play them on strings 5 through 3 and 6 through 4, and to change them to minor, diminished, and augmented triads. Be sure to play through all keys in the same way. You should also play through this exercise using the other voicings you have learned, including the open voicings (three-note chords on non-consecutive strings) and voicings which include doubling.

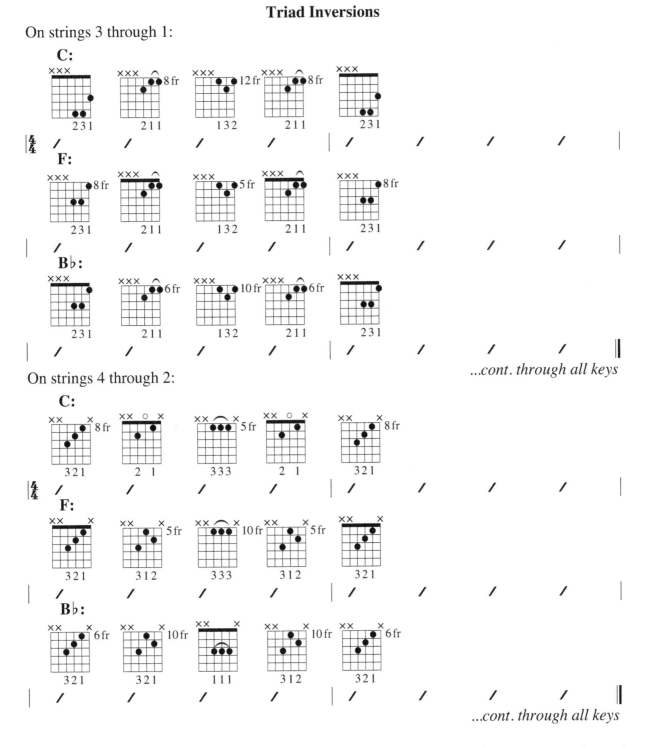

Triad Inversions

On strings 3 through 1:

On strings 4 through 2:

...cont. through all keys

Note: When practicing augmented chords, the shape stays the same. It simply moves up or down the fingerboard four frets for each inversion.

Exercise 2 — Inversions Over the Entire Fingerboard

This exercise works you through triad inversions running up and down the entire fingerboard, starting with the lowest playable inversion. The example given uses strings 3, 2, and 1, with the major triads C, F, and Bb. You should continue through all remaining keys. Do the same with the rest of the three-note triads using other strings, including non-consecutive groups. Also change them to minor, diminished, and augmented.

Triad Inversions–Entire Fingerboard

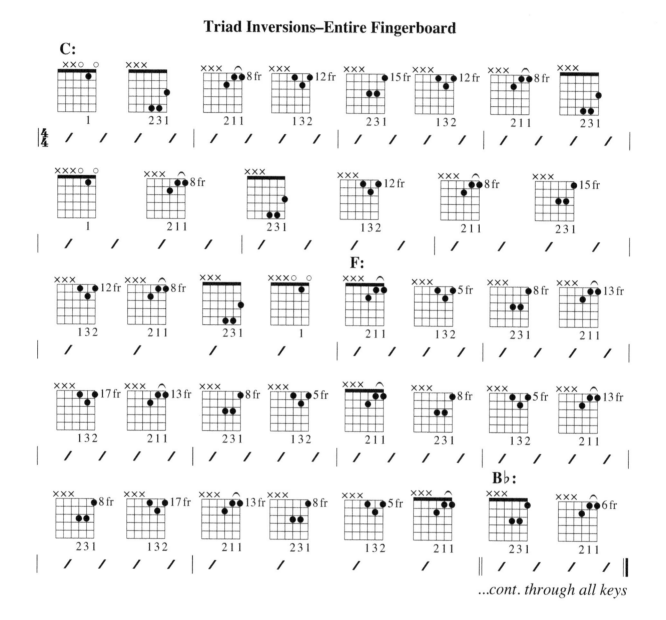

...cont. through all keys

Exercise 3 — I–IV–V Chords, Close Groupings

This exercise runs through I–IV–V progressions in all possible positions, using inversions of those chords which are close to each other. Be sure to run through this exercise with the voicings that are omitted, both major and minor, and transpose to all keys. Don't use the diminished or augmented chords here.

Major I–IV–V Triads–Key of C

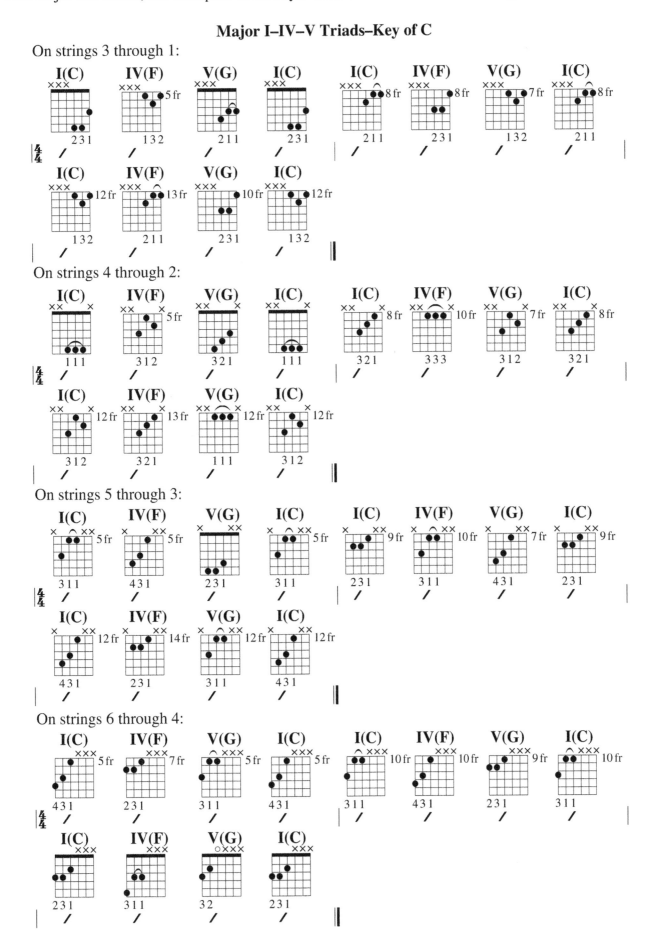

On strings 3 through 1:

On strings 4 through 2:

On strings 5 through 3:

On strings 6 through 4:

Minor i–iv–v Triads–Key of C Minor

On strings 3 through 1:

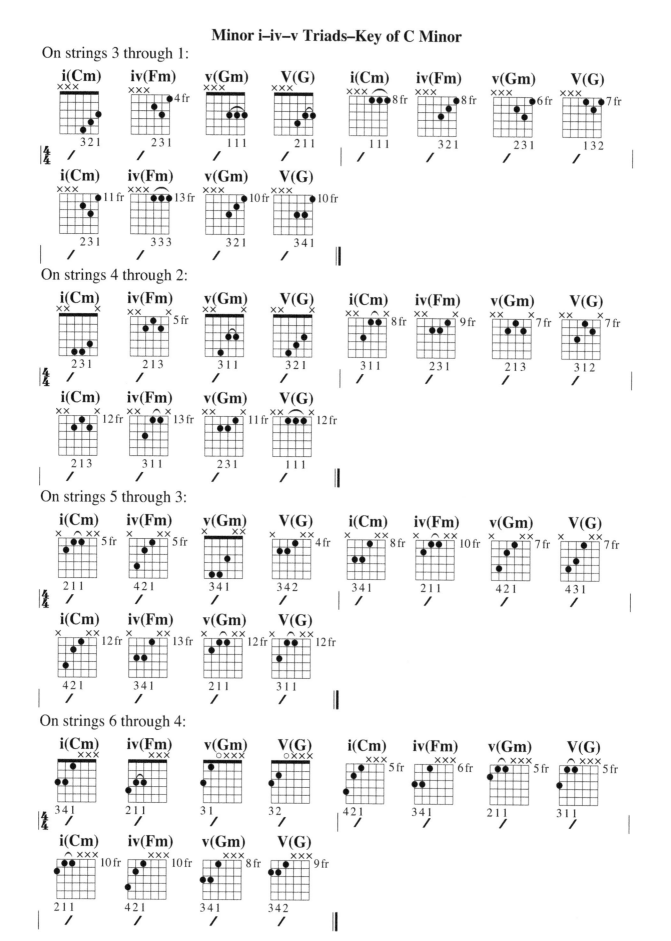

On strings 4 through 2:

On strings 5 through 3:

On strings 6 through 4:

Note: The above minor i–iv–v exercises include a major V chord because in a minor blues progression we would use it in the turnaround, if not for any other occurrence.

After you have worked through the preceding I–IV–V chord exercises, try playing through a twelve-bar blues progression, or any other three-chord rock or R&B tunes you know, using the groupings you've just learned.

Exercise 4 — Diminished Chords

This exercise shows you ways you can use the diminished triad as a ii° chord in a minor key. It oscillates between the i chord and the ii° chord.

Diminished Chords–Key of G Minor

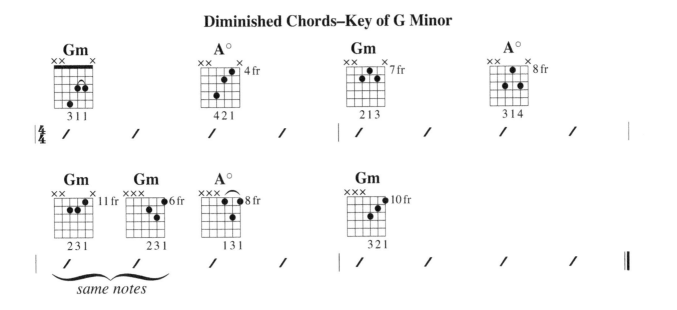

same notes

Exercise 5 — Augmented V Chords

Here is a way to use the augmented triad in a minor i–IV–V progression.

Augmented Chords–Key of G Minor

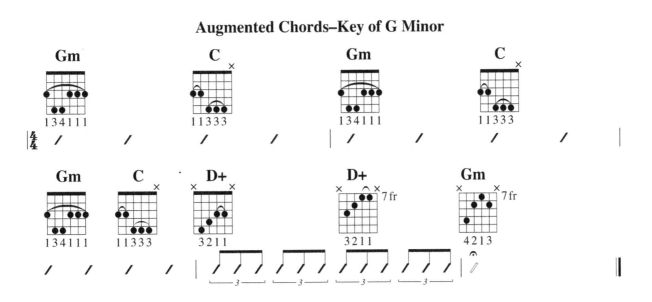

Exercise 6 — Twelve-Bar Blues

Here are two examples that use major triads in a twelve-bar blues progression. While seventh and ninth chords are usually favored over straight triads in the blues, triads can be used.

Closed Voice Twelve-Bar Blues–Key of C

Open Voice Twelve-Bar Blues–Key of A

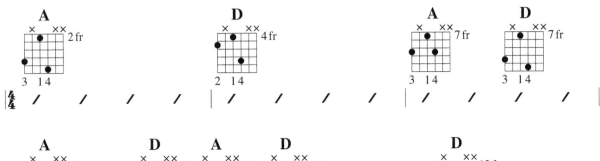

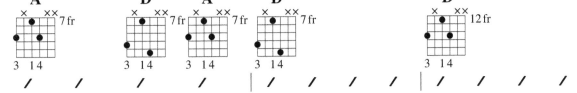

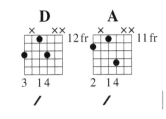

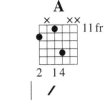

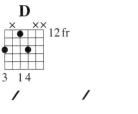

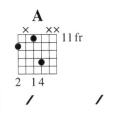

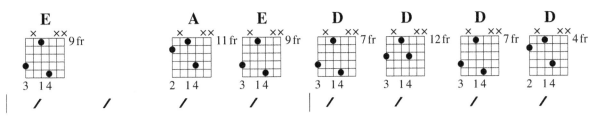

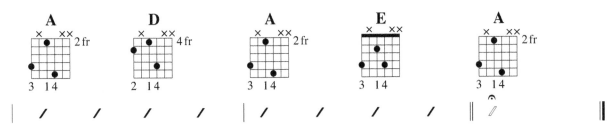

Exercise 7 — Rock-Style I–IV–V Progression

Here's a I–IV–V progression in a rock style.

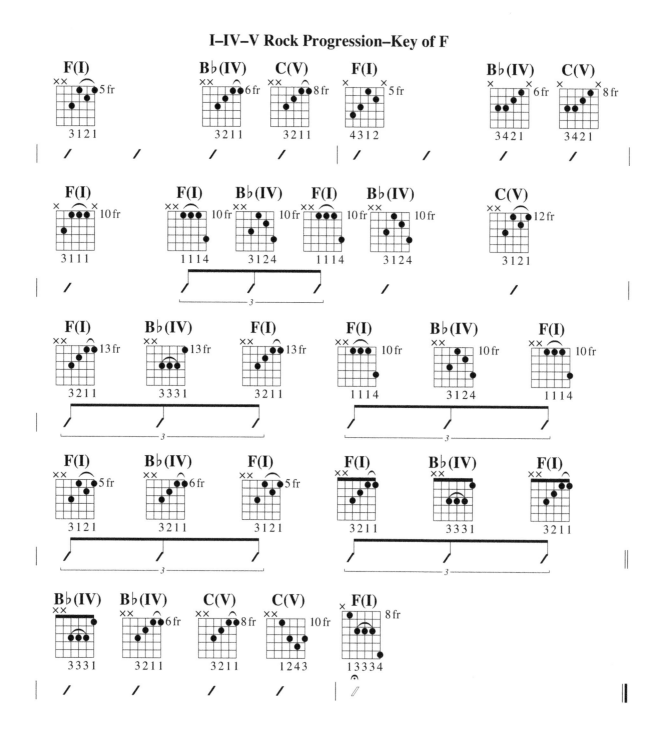

I–IV–V Rock Progression–Key of F

For fun, try the following variations on the above progression:

- Change the whole progression to minor.
- Change the whole progression to minor, keeping the V chord major.
- Change the whole progression to minor, but make the V chord augmented.

Exercise 8 — Minor Twelve-Bar Blues Progression

This exercise is a twelve-bar blues progression in G minor.

Minor Twelve-Bar Blues–Key of G Minor

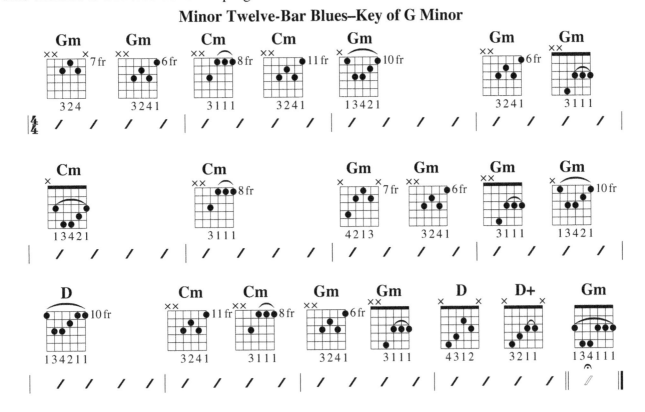

Exercise 9 — Minor and Major Combination

This chord progression makes use of major and minor, as well as augmented chords. It is not a twelve-bar blues progression. Instead, it is as follows:

Major and Minor Combination–Key of G Minor

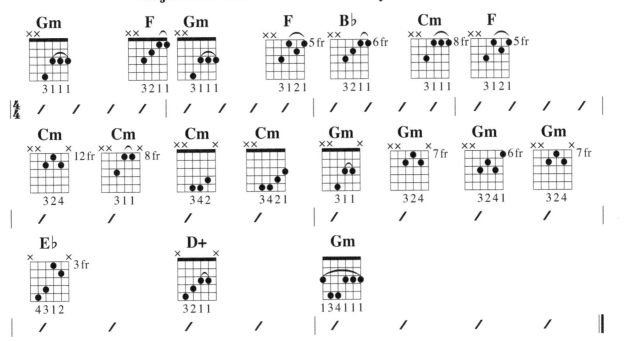

Exercise 10 — "Bluesy" Rock Progression

Here's a "bluesy" type of rock progression. It is given in two different keys (to show how a small change is sometimes needed to fit another key), and yet it retains the same flavor in both keys. The progression is as follows:

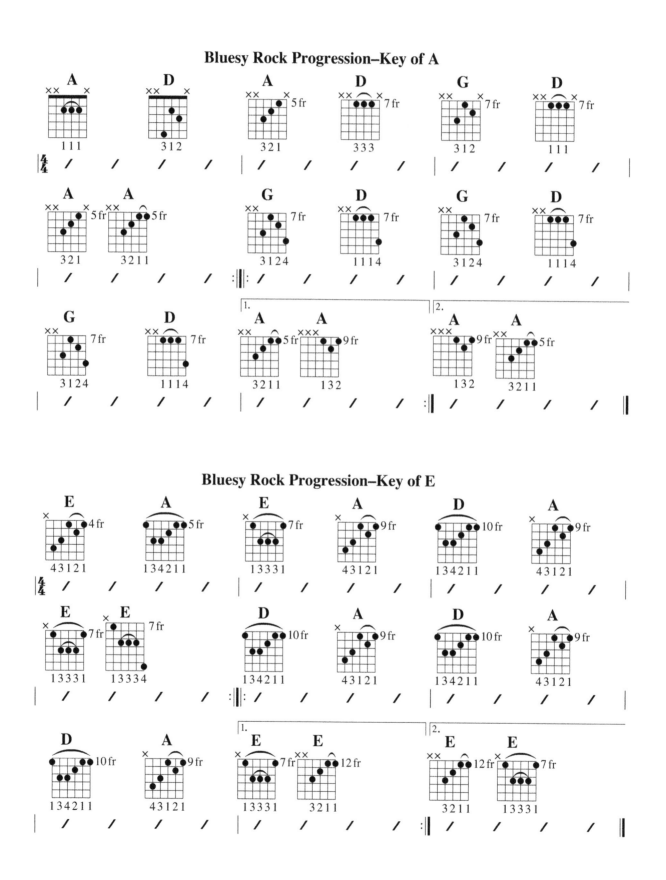

Seventh Chords

Exercise 1 — Inversions

For this exercise, go back and look at Exercises 1 and 2 of the Triads section, and follow the same procedures but with major, dominant, and minor seventh chords. There is one more inversion of the seventh chords than with triads, since sevenths contain four notes. They are laid out in the CHORDS section, by inversion, so there shouldn't be any confusion.

Exercise 2 — I7–IV7–V7 Chords, Close Groupings

This exercise gives you some I7–IV7–V7 chord groupings, with the voicings close together, as you had in the Triads section. Use each of the groupings in a twelve-bar progression. You'll see they offer very smooth voice leading from chord to chord. Notice the arrow on the left side of the diagrams; it is always pointing to the same fret. Play these chord forms in every key.

I^7–IV^7–V^7 Chord Groupings

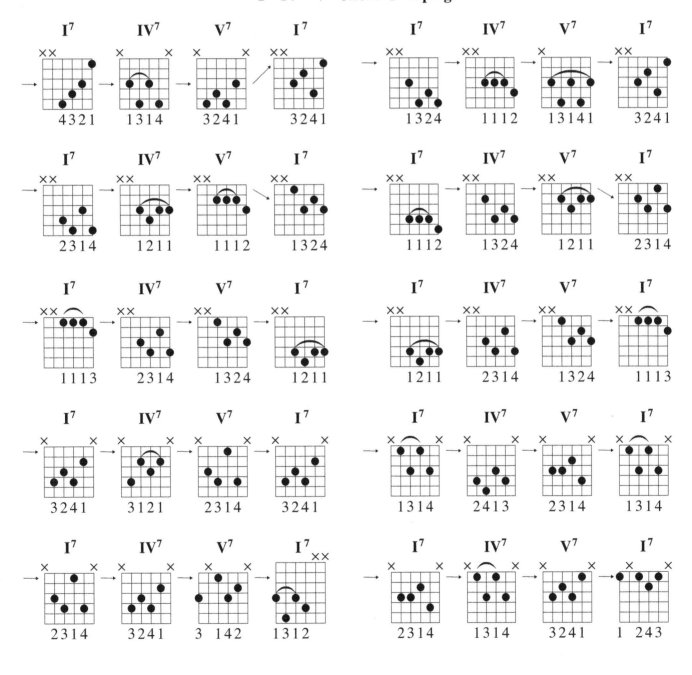

Exercise 3 — ii7–V7–Imaj7 Progression, Close Groupings

Another very important progression in the blues, as well as in jazz and R&B, is the ii7–V7–Imaj7 progression. This exercise gives you some examples using the principle of smooth voice leading.

ii7–V7–Imaj7 Progression

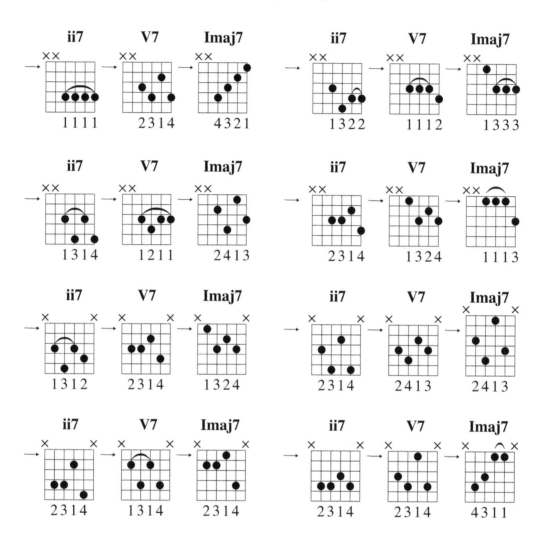

Exercise 4 — Twelve-Bar Blues

Here's an example of using dominant seventh chords in the blues.

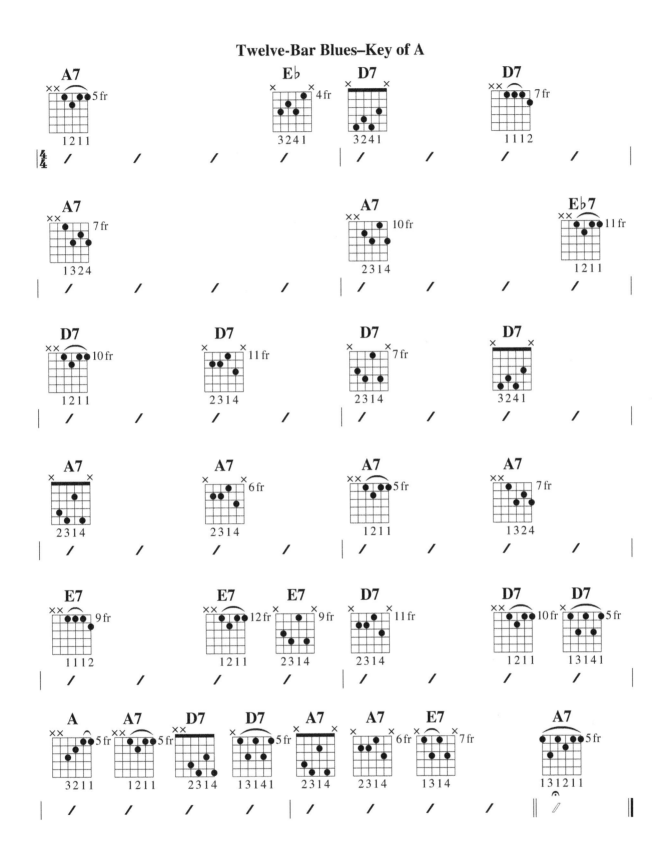

Twelve-Bar Blues–Key of A

Exercise 5 — Twelve-Bar Blues with Secondary Chords

This is an example of the use of dominant seventh chords and minor sevenths (as secondary chords) in a blues progression similar to the famous "Stormy Monday."

Twelve-Bar Blues with Dominant and Minor Seventh Chords–Key of G

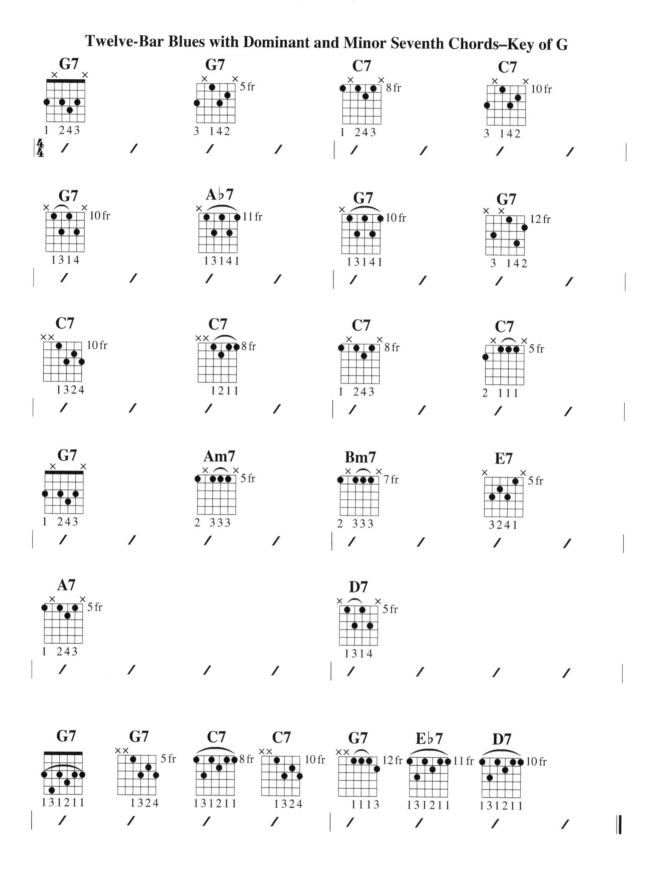

Exercise 6 — Minor Blues

This is a minor blues progression using mostly minor seventh chords.

Minor Blues Progression–Key of C Minor

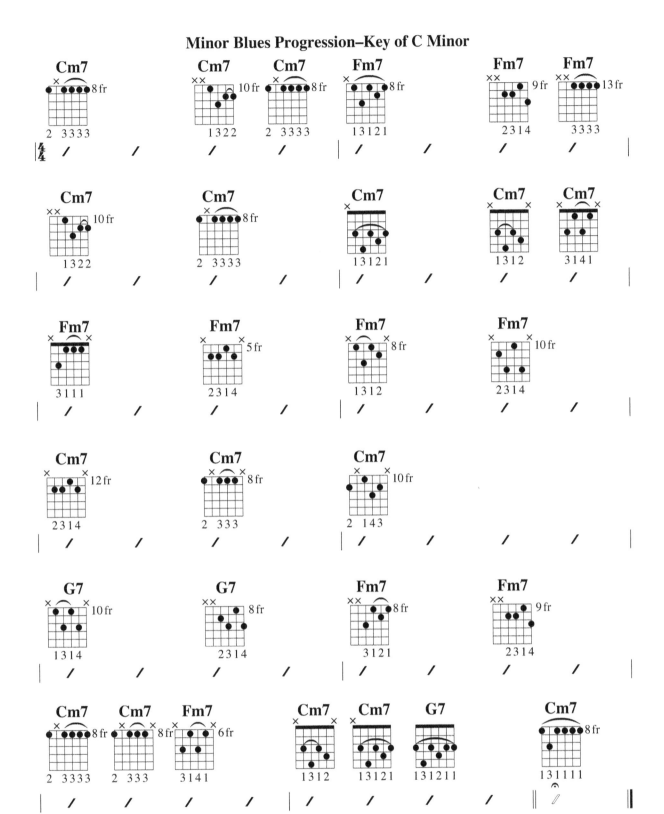

Exercise 7 — Jazz-Style Blues with Major Seventh Chords

This last exercise shows how a jazz-style blues progression makes use of major seventh chords, as well as of dominant and minor sevenths.

Jazz-Style Twelve-Bar Blues–Key of B♭

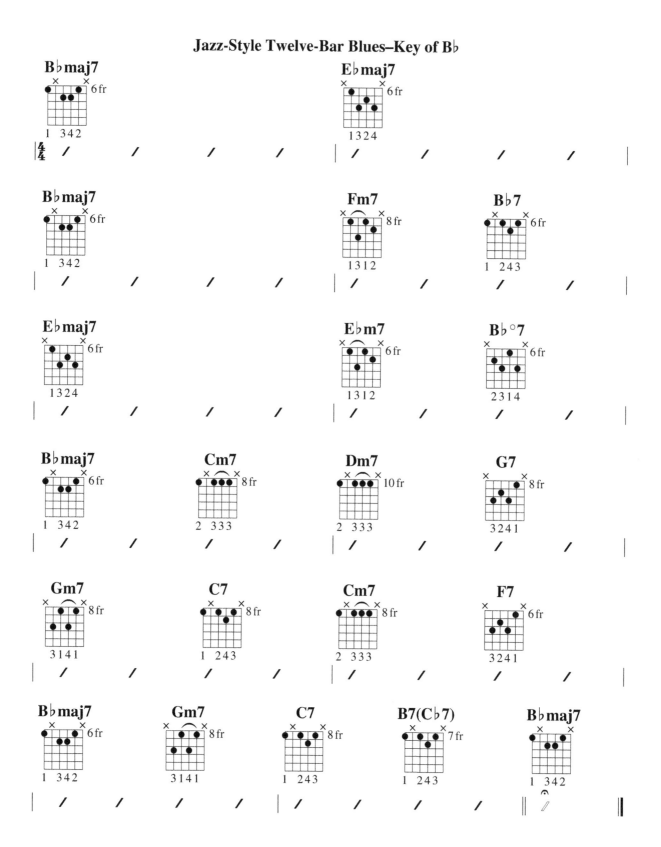

Diminished Seventh Chords

Exercise 1 — Inversions

This exercise runs through diminished seventh chords, up and down the neck, much in the same way as the first two triad and seventh chord exercises. Remember, any one of the four notes of the chord can be the root!

Diminished Seventh Chord Inversions

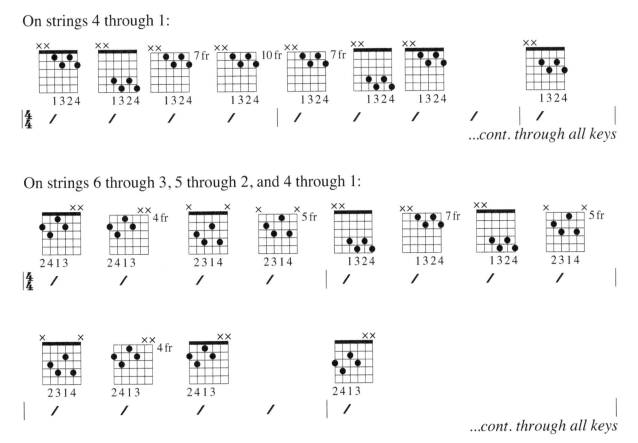

On strings 4 through 1:

On strings 6 through 3, 5 through 2, and 4 through 1:

...cont. through all keys

Exercise 2 — Resolution to I7 Chord

This exercise shows some possible resolutions to the I7 chord of the indicated keys. Here, the diminished seventh chords are considered to be the #IV dim7 of the key. Be sure to try these resolutions in all keys.

Diminished Seventh Chord Resolutions

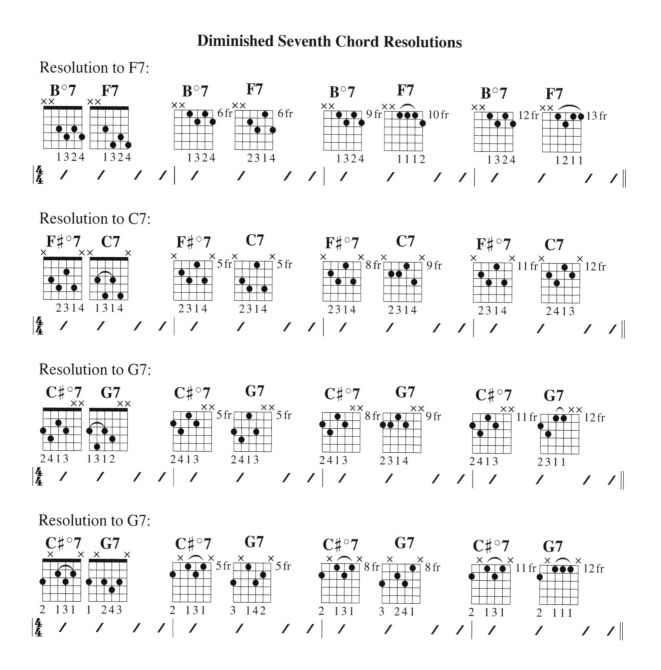

Exercise 3 — Passing Chords in Twelve-Bar Blues

Here's how you might use diminished sevenths as passing chords in a twelve-bar blues progression. The diminished chords are the #IV of the key, as they were in the previous exercise. This example begins with a four-bar intro, starting with the V7 chord.

Diminished Seventh Passing Chords–Key of A

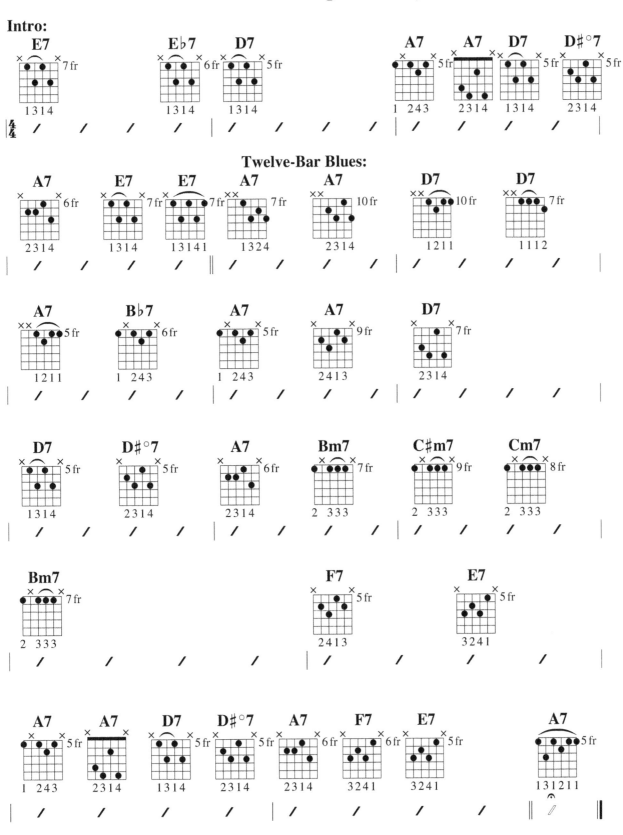

Exercise 4 — More Passing Chords in the Blues

Here's another example using diminished seventh passing chords in the blues. In this tune, the diminished seventh chords resolve to more than just the I7 chord, but in all cases they resolve as though the chord to which they are moving is the I7 of a new key. Just think of that chord as the key of the tune, temporarily, and the diminished seventh chord as the ♯IV of that temporary key. For example, where you have a G♯°7 in measure 8 resolving to a D7 in the next bar, think of the progression as temporarily being in the key of D.

More Diminished Seventh Passing Chords–Key of G

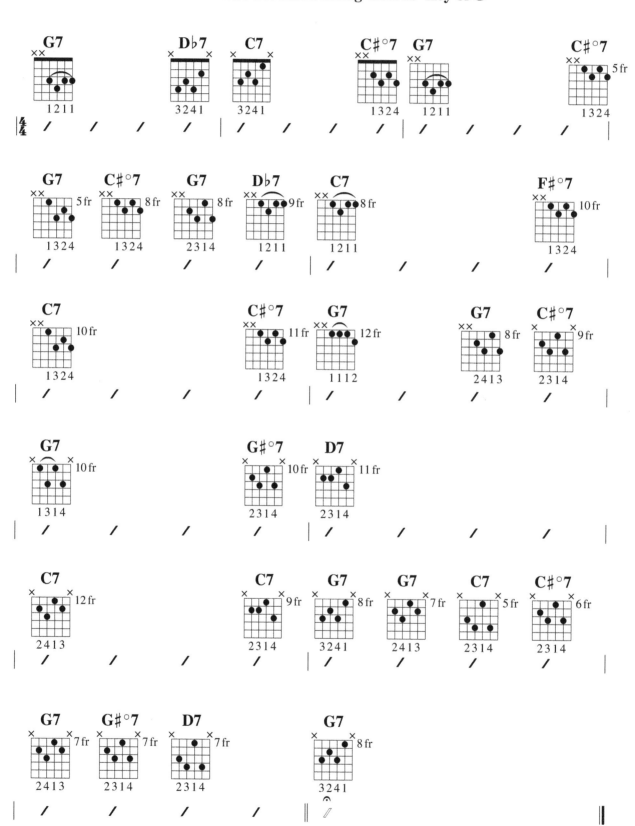

Sixth Chords

Exercise 1 — Twelve-Bar Blues

This is an example of the use of sixth chords in the blues.

Twelve-Bar Blues with Sixth Chords–Key of G

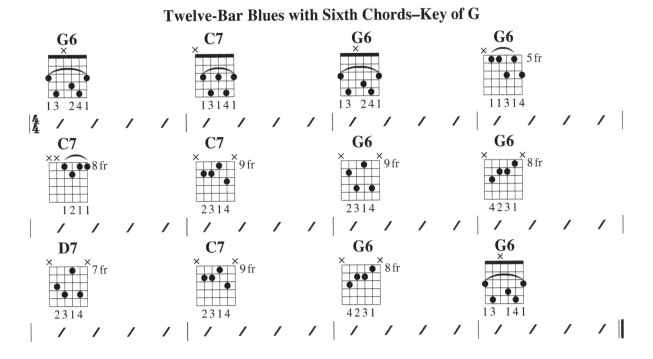

Exercise 2 — Minor Twelve-Bar Blues

Here's a minor blues progression using minor sixth and minor seventh chords.

Minor Blues with Minor Sixths and Minor Sevenths–Key of D Minor

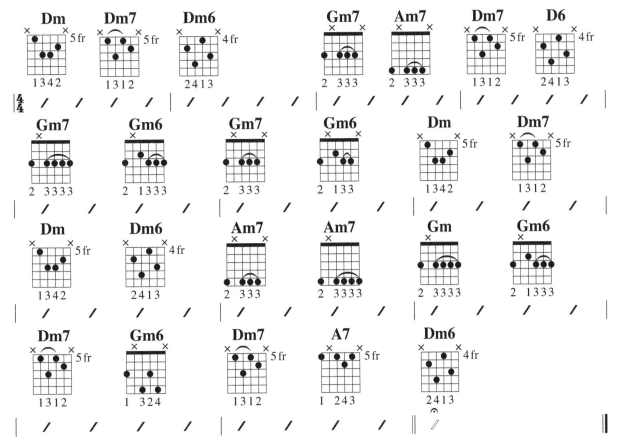

Ninth Chords

Exercise 1 — I9–IV9–V9 Chords, Close Groupings

This exercise gives you some I9–IV9–V9 groupings close together on the fingerboard, as you practiced with triads and seventh chords. Find as many more groupings as you can.

Dominant Ninth Chord Groupings

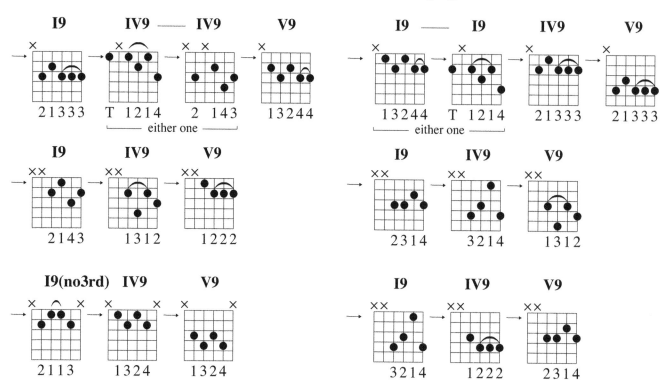

Exercise 2 — ii9–V9–IM9 Progression, Close Groupings

Here are some groupings for a ii9–V9–Imaj9 progression, similar to the ii7–V7–Imaj7 progression you learned in the seventh chord section. These two progressions function the same and are interchangeable. Note some of the I chords in this progression are Imaj7 chords. It is perfectly acceptable to mix seventh and ninth chords of the same type (major, minor, or dominant).

ii9–V9–Imaj9 (or maj7) Groupings

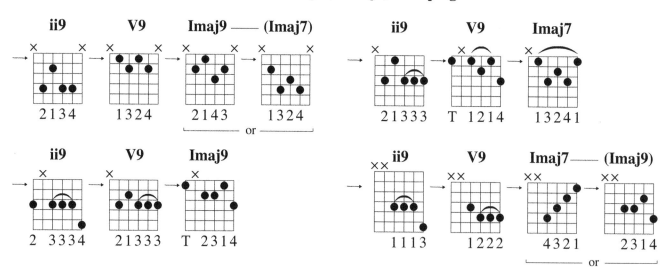

Exercise 3 — Simple Twelve-Bar Blues

This exercise makes use of ninth chords in a simple twelve-bar blues progression.

Simple Twelve-Bar Blues–Key of A

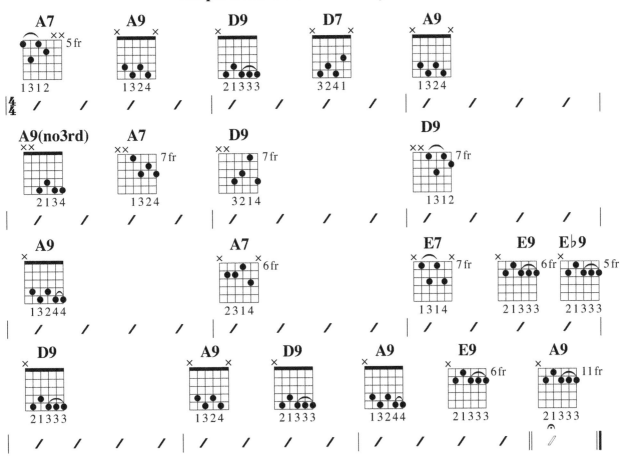

Exercise 4 — Twelve-Bar Blues

Here's another simple twelve-bar blues using ninth chords.

Simple Twelve-Bar Blues–Key of E

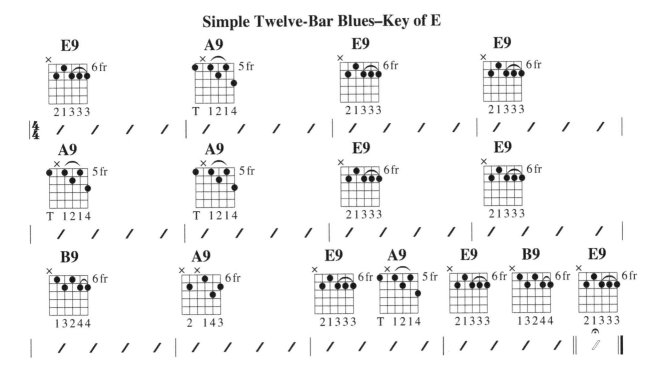

Exercise 5 — Twelve-Bar Blues, Embellished

Here's a twelve-bar blues progression using ninth chords in place of sevenths. Notice how you can slide into each of the I9, IV9, and V9 chords from a fret above or below. You'll find that this is an easy and effective way to fill out and "fancy up" your rhythm playing.

Twelve-Bar Blues–Key of C

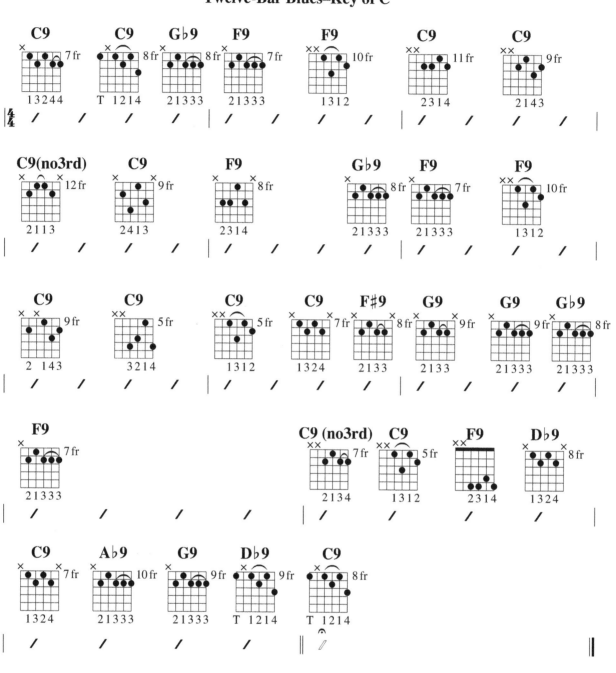

Exercise 6 — Twelve-Bar Blues with Secondary Chords

This progression uses secondary chords (ii, iii, and ♭iii) as in earlier exercises. In this case, some of those secondary chords are minor ninth chords, which are interchangeable with minor sevenths.

Twelve-Bar Blues–Key of G

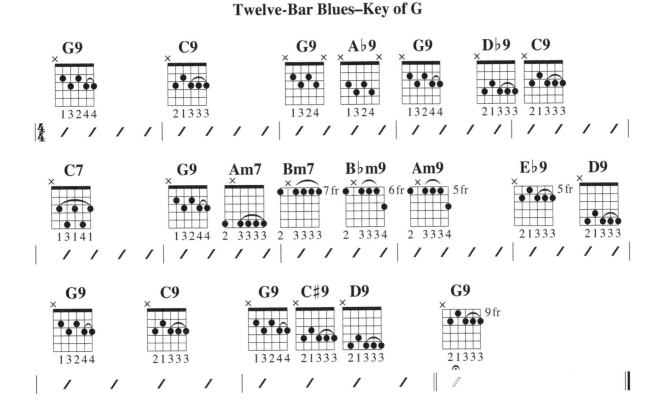

Exercise 7 — Minor Blues

Here is an example of a minor blues progression using minor seventh and minor ninth chords mixed together.

Minor Blues–Key of A Minor

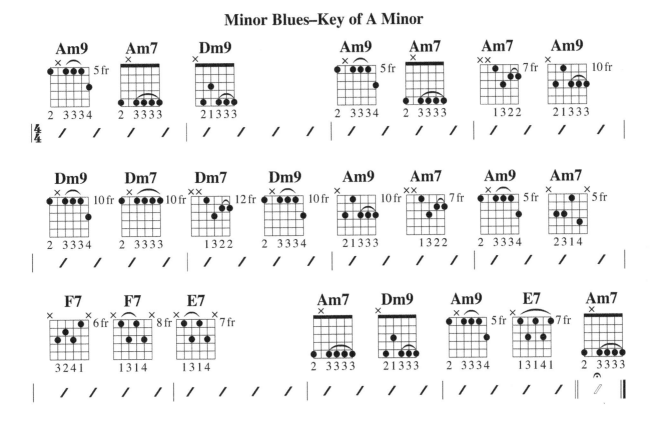

Eleventh, sus4 and 7Sus4 Chords

Exercise 1 — Eleventh Chord Resolutions

This exercise takes you through four keys using dominant eleventh chords.

Eleventh Chord Resolutions

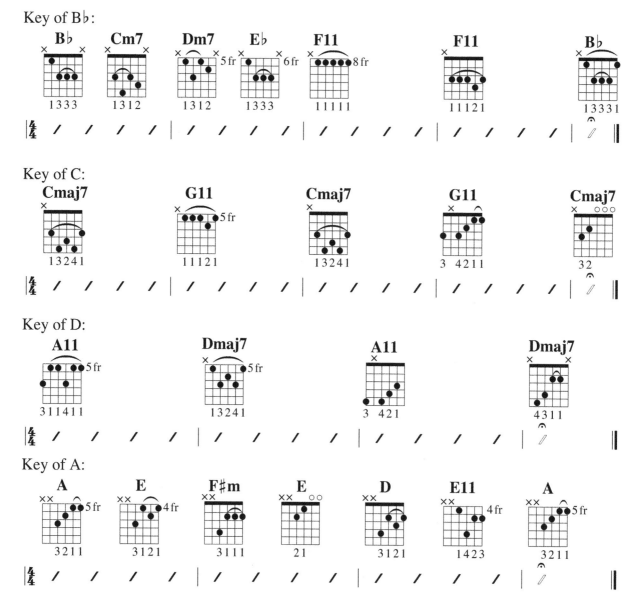

Exercise 2 — Sus4 and 7sus4 Chord Resolutions

This is a simple example of the use of sus4 and 7sus4 chords.

Sus4 and 7sus4 Chord Resolutions–Key of E♭

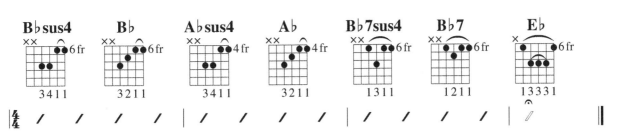

There will be more examples of the use of eleventh and 7sus4 chords in the following sections.

Thirteenth Chords

Exercise 1 — Simple Twelve-Bar Blues

This exercise gives you an idea of how to use thirteenth chords in a simple twelve-bar blues tune.

Simple Twelve-Bar Blues–Key of A

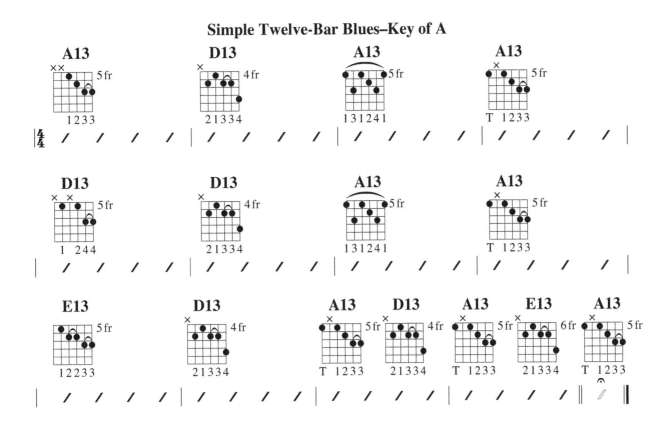

Exercise 2 — Ninth and Thirteenth Chords in Twelve-Bar Blues

Here is an example of combining ninth and thirteenth chords to get some interesting sounds in a twelve-bar blues tune.

Twelve-Bar Blues–Key of C

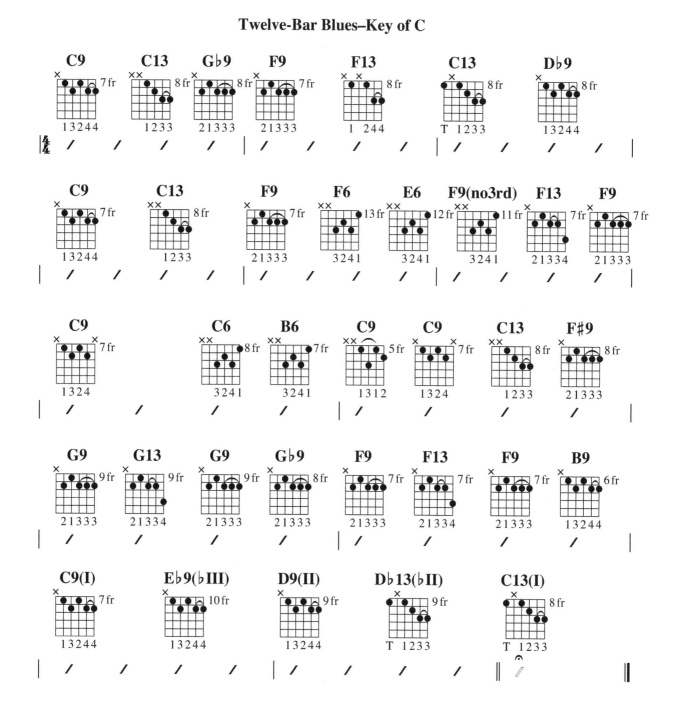

Exercise 3 — Creating Melody with Chords in the Blues

Now that you have advanced to thirteenth chords, you will see how combining sevenths, ninths, and thirteenths can give you a lot of freedom in creating melodies with chords. Here's an example.

Melody Blues–Key of A

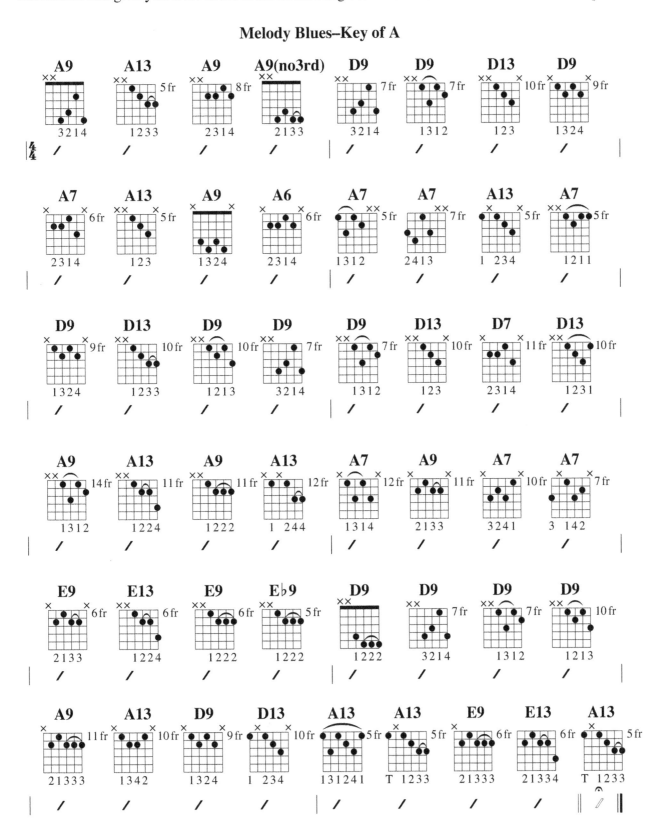

As an additional exercise, try going back through the previous examples of blues progressions and replace seventh or ninth chords with thirteenths. You will find this often will work well, though sometimes thirteenths just don't fit the tune.

Altered Chords

Exercise 1 — ii7♭5–V7♯9(or ♭9)–i7

This exercise contains some examples of a ii–V–i progression in a minor key. The chord types used are ii7♭5, V7♯9 or ♭9, and i7 or i9.

ii7♭5–V7(♭ or ♯9)–i7(or 9) Progression–Key of G Minor

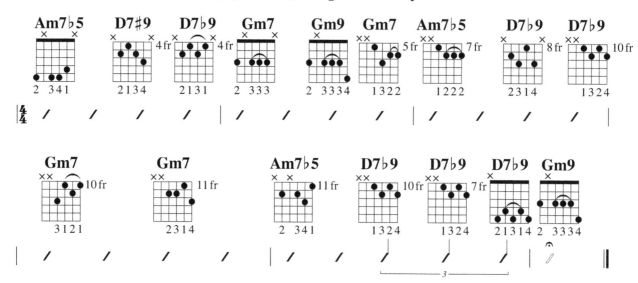

Exercise 2 — Basic Twelve-Bar Blues Using Altered Ninth Chords

Here's a fairly basic twelve-bar blues making use of altered ninth chords.

Twelve-Bar Blues with Altered Chords–Key of A

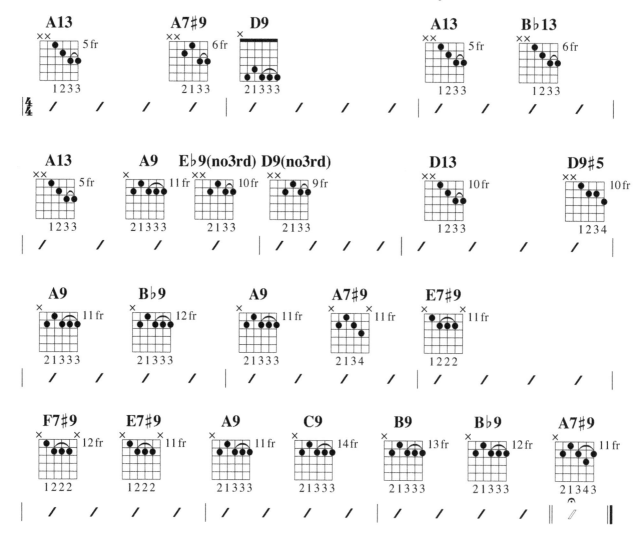

Exercise 3 — Twelve-Bar Blues with Secondary Chords

This is an example of a variation on the "Stormy Monday" type progression we saw earlier, using altered ninth chords.

Twelve-Bar Blues–Key of G

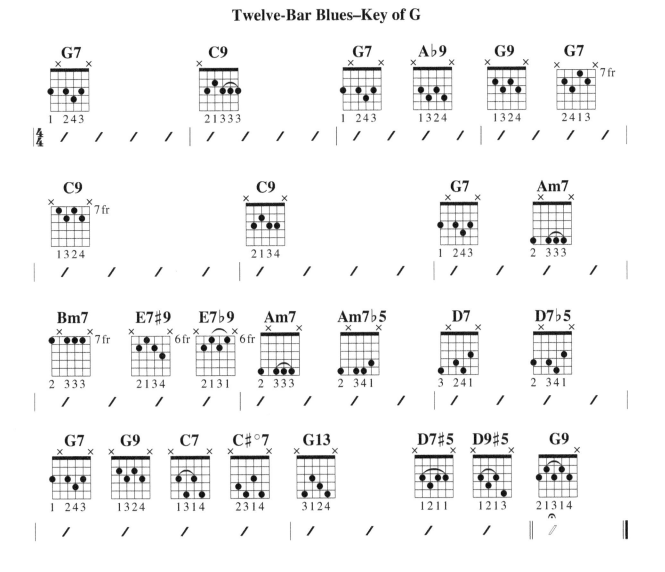

Exercise 4 — Chords with Multiple Altered Notes in a Twelve-Bar Blues

This progression uses some of the more complex altered chords, like 7♭5♭9 and minor 7♭5 chords. The progression, while a twelve-bar blues, gets fairly complex. Notice how the voices flow from one chord to the next.

Twelve-Bar Blues–Key of C

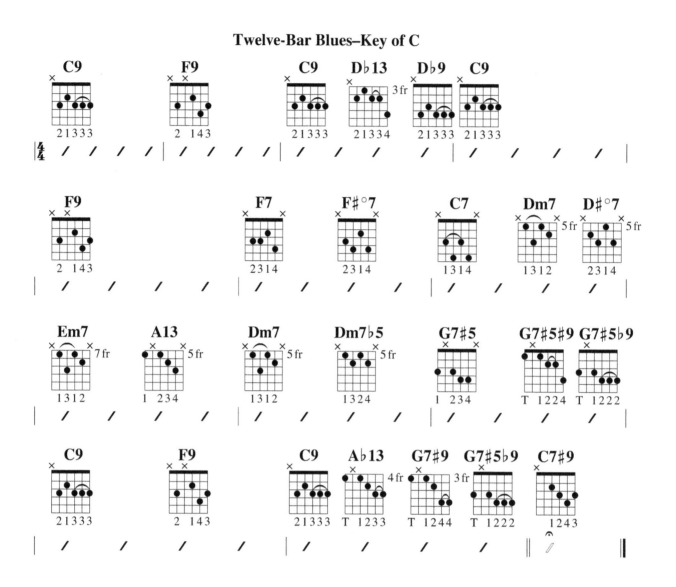

Exercise 5 — Minor Blues Progression

Here is a minor blues progression making use of altered chords. It's fairly jazz-like.

Twelve-Bar Minor Blues–Key of A

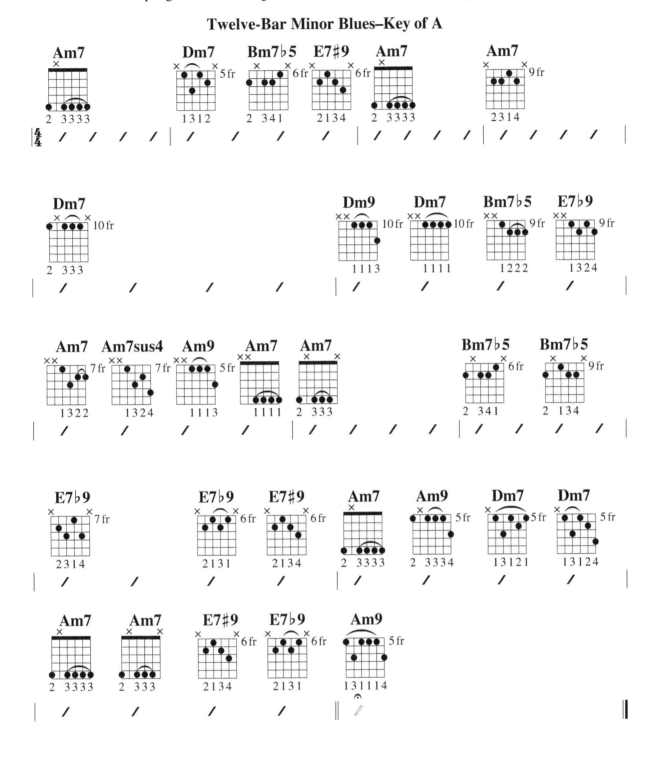

Exercise 6 — Rock-Style Blues with I7♯9

Here's a simpler progression in more of a rock style. It makes use of a I7♯9 chord.

Blues/Rock Progression with I7♯9 Chords–Key of E

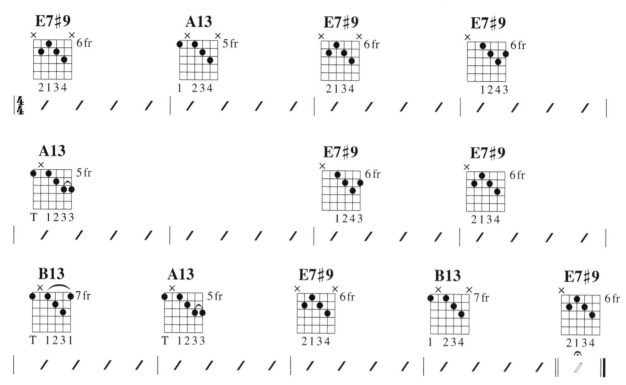

Exercise 7 — Simple Jazz-Style Blues with Imaj7 and IVmaj7 Chords

This is an example of a simple jazz-style blues progression. It uses a major seventh for the I and IV chords. The turnaround (the last two bars) is a I–vi–ii–V type. See *Blues You Can Use* for a detailed explanation of turnarounds.

Simple Jazz-Style Blues–Key of C

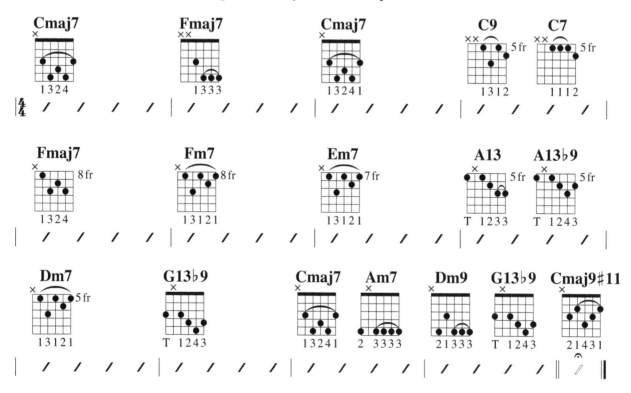

Exercise 8 — Complex Jazz-Style Blues—Lots of ii–V's

In this example, a more complex jazz-style blues progression is given. See if you can find the ii–V progressions throughout in different keys. This is how a jazz player would see it.

Jazz-Style Blues–Key of B♭

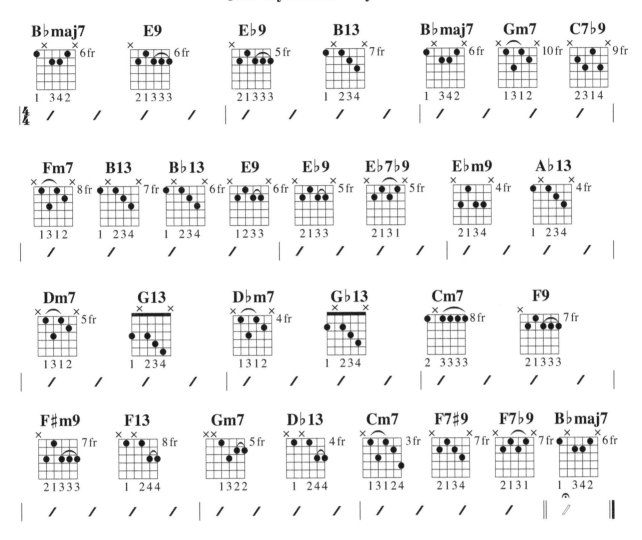

Other Chords

Exercise 1 — Simple Jazz-Style Blues Using Major 6/9 Chords

Here's a simple jazz-style blues, much like the one in the previous section, using major 6/9 chords in place of the major sevenths.

Simple Jazz-Style Blues–Key of C

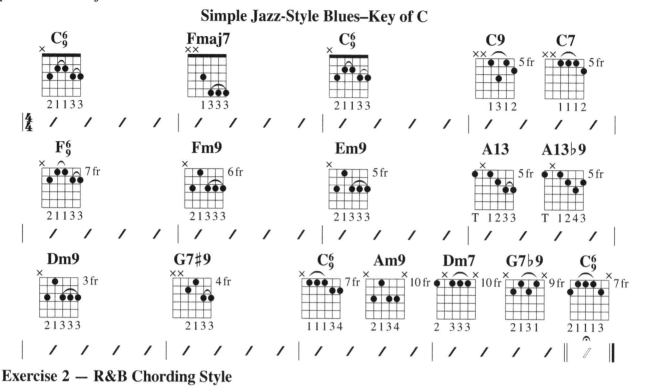

Exercise 2 — R&B Chording Style

This is an example of the use of chords you have learned, played in an R&B chording style.

R&B Chord Style–Key of A

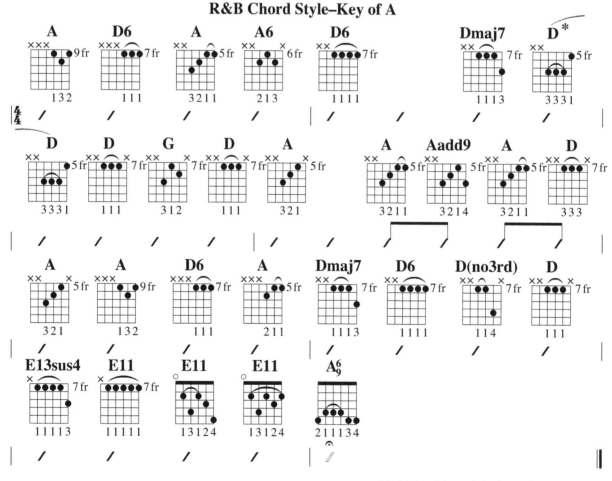

* hold chord through 1st beat of next measure.

Exercise 3 — Using Minor-Major Seventh Chords

Here are a few examples of the use of minor-major sevenths as passing chords. The progression is from a minor triad to a major-minor seventh to a minor seventh, and finally to a minor sixth chord, all with the same root. The only movement is the line from the root through the ♮7th and ♭7th to the 6th.

Minor-Major Seventh Passing Chords

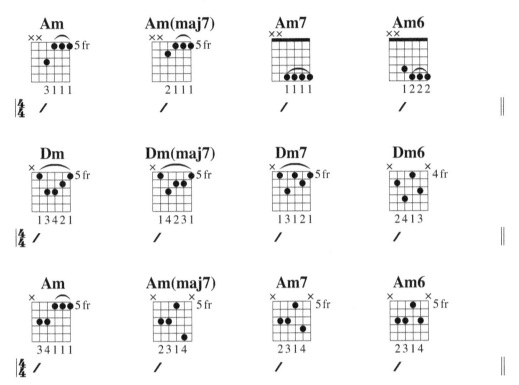

Exercise 4 — R&B Ballad Style

This final exercise illustrates a basic modern R&B ballad style, making use of the add9 and minor-major seventh chords.

Modern R&B Ballad Style–Key of C

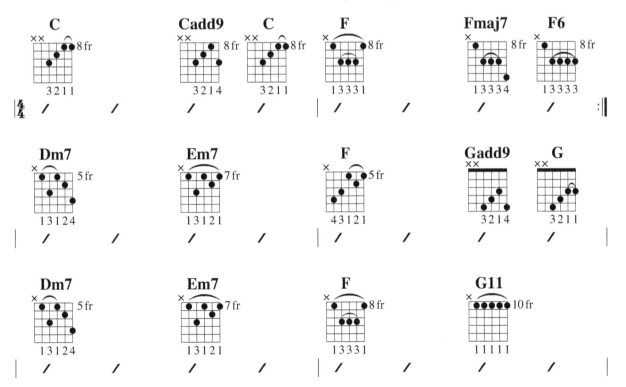

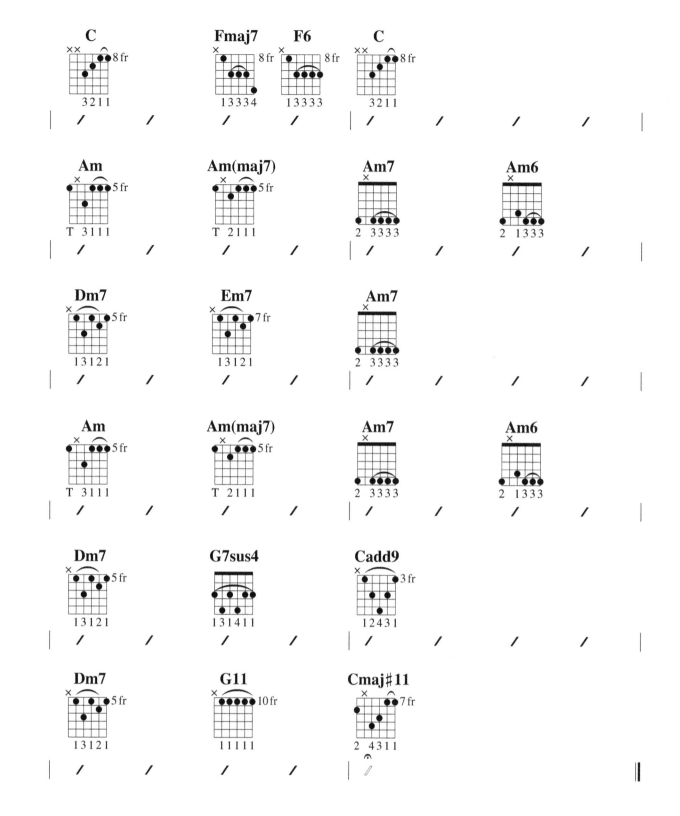

WHERE TO GO FROM HERE

This book is meant to be as complete a reference as possible while still remaining true to its focus—chords you can use for blues-based music. While other chords are possible (remember, a chord is defined as three different notes—*any* three different notes), the ones we have covered in this book constitute virtually all those which can conceivably be used in the blues and blues-based music, and then some.

There are systems other than the tertian harmony system from which you can construct chords—the quartal harmony system, for example, where chords are built from 4ths instead of 3rds. If you are interested in delving more deeply into those possibilities, I strongly encourage you to look into harmony books at your local library. Don't rely on guitar books alone, but rather, check out jazz keyboard harmony books (John Mehagan has a series which is great) and general theory books (*Popular and Jazz Harmony* by Daniel Ricigliano is very good).

I would also encourage those of you who are serious about a professional career in music to study at a good music school or with a private teacher who is well-versed in theory.

As for the application of these chords in your playing, you can refer to the other books in the *BLUES YOU CAN USE* series for specific rhythm guitar styles in the blues and blues-based genres. Also, listen, listen, and listen to blues, rock, R&B, and jazz recordings for ideas. Listen not only to the rhythm and lead guitar parts, but also to the piano and other keyboard parts as well. You may not be able to play exactly what keyboard players do, but you can get great ideas from them.

SECTION 4: APPENDIX

Chord Nomenclature (Symbols)

These are the commonly used symbols for the various chords.
All examples are given in the key of C.

Major triad:	C, C Maj, C Ma, CM, C△
Minor triad:	Cm, C min, C mi, C-
Diminished triad:	C°, C dim
Augmented triad:	C+, Caug, C+5

Major 7th:	Cmaj7, C Ma7, CM7, C△7, C♮7 (European)
Minor 7th:	Cm7, C min7, C mi7, C-7
Dominant 7th:	C7, C♭7 (European)

Diminished 7th:	C°7, C dim7, Cd7

Major 6th:	C6
Minor 6th:	Cm6, C min6, C mi6, C-6

Major 9th:	Cmaj9, C Ma9, CM9, C△9
Minor 9th:	Cm9, C min9, C mi9, C-9
Dominant 9th:	C9

Dominant 11th:	C11
Minor 11th:	Cm11, C min11, C mi11, C-11

Dominant 13th:	C13
Minor 13th:	Cm13, C min13, C mi13, C-13

Dominant 7♭5:	C7♭5
Minor 7♭5:	Cm7♭5, C min7♭5, C mi7♭5, C-7♭5, C∅7 (for half-diminished 7th)
Dominant 7♯5:	C7♯5, C7+5, Caug7 (for augmented 7th)
Dominant 7♯9:	C7♯9, C7+9
Dominant 7♭9:	C7♭9, C7-9
Major 7♯11:	Cmaj7♯11, C Maj7+11, C Ma7♯11, C Ma7+11, CM7♯11, CM7+11, C△7♯11, C△7+11

Note: For chords with multiple altered notes, follow the standard used for the seventh chord contained within, and then list the altered notes.

Examples: C7♭5♭9, Cm7♭5♭9, C7♯5♭9, C7♭5♯9

Notes of the Scales

These scales may be used to build chords, as shown in the THEORY section of this book.

Major scales

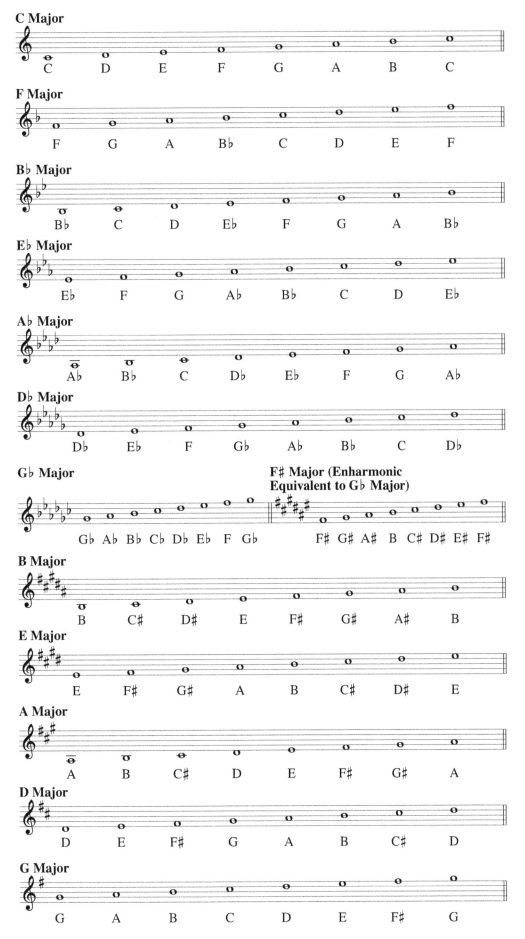

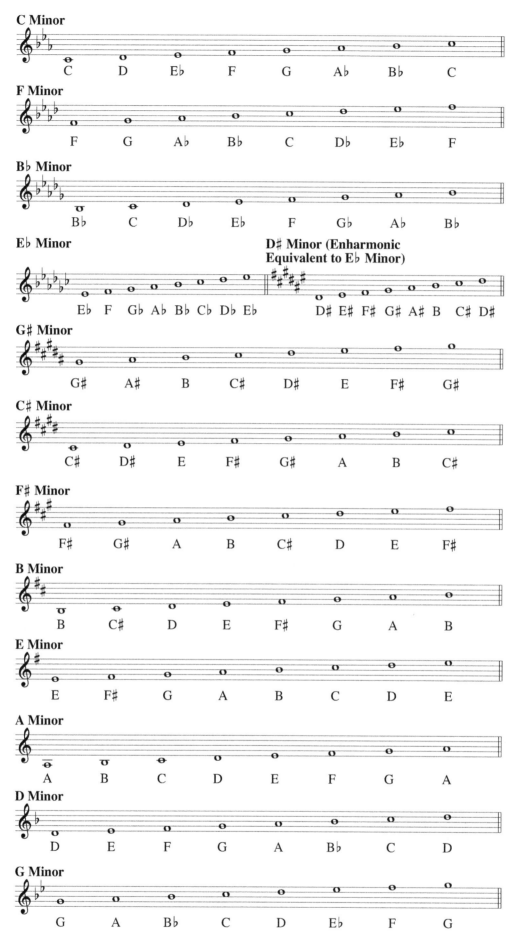

Chords in Each Key

This section lists the chords found in the various types of keys discussed in this book.

The primary chords of each key (I, IV, and V) are separated from the secondary chords (ii, iii, vi, and viiⱺ) because, in blues and rock, the primary chords are often the only chords used.

The chord types are given as seventh chords. You can convert them to triads of the same basic type (e.g., major, minor, and diminished). You may also convert them to extended chords such as ninths, thirteenths, etc. Just remember to keep the type the same (e.g., major, minor, dominant, or minor ♭5) and follow the guidelines given for the use of each type in the THEORY section. The basic rule of thumb is you may interchange between all chords of the same type, as long as there is no clash with any other players or with the melody—you'll know right away if there is a clash by the way it sounds.

The chords may also be altered, using the guidelines given to you in the Altered Chords chapter, and, most of all, using your ear.

Blues Keys (Used for Non-Minor Blues):

Key	Primary chords			Secondary chords			
	I	IV	V	ii	iii	vi	♭VII
C	C7	F7	G7	Dm7	Em7	Am7	B♭7
F	F7	B♭7	C7	Gm7	Am7	Dm7	E♭7
B♭	B♭7	E♭7	F7	Cm7	Dm7	Gm7	A♭7
E♭	E♭7	A♭7	B♭7	Fm7	Gm7	Cm7	D♭7
A♭	A♭7	D♭7	E♭7	B♭m7	Cm7	Fm7	G♭7
D♭ (C♯)	D♭7	G♭7	A♭7	E♭m7	Fm7	B♭m7	C♭7
F♯	F♯7	B7	C♯7	G♯m7	A♯m7	D♯m7	E7
B	B7	E7	F♯7	C♯m7	D♯m7	G♯m7	A7
E	E7	A7	B7	F♯m7	G♯m7	C♯m7	D7
A	A7	D7	E7	Bm7	C♯m7	F♯m7	G7
D	D7	G7	A7	Em7	F♯m7	Bm7	C7
G	G7	C7	D7	Am7	Bm7	Em7	F7

Major Keys (Used for R&B, Rock, Blues-Rock and Jazz-Style Blues):

Key	Primary chords			Secondary chords			
	I	IV	V	ii	iii	vi	viiⱺ
C	Cmaj7	Fmaj7	G7	Dm7	Em7	Am7	Bm7♭5
F	Fmaj7	B♭maj7	C7	Gm7	Am7	Dm7	Em7♭5
B♭	B♭maj7	E♭maj7	F7	Cm7	Dm7	Gm7	Am7♭5
E♭	E♭maj7	A♭maj7	B♭7	Fm7	Gm7	Cm7	Dm7♭5
A♭	A♭maj7	D♭maj7	E♭7	B♭m7	Cm7	Fm7	Gm7♭5
D♭ (C♯)	D♭maj7	G♭maj7	A♭7	E♭m7	Fm7	B♭m7	Cm7♭5
F♯	F♯maj7	Bmaj7	C♯7	G♯m7	A♯m7	D♯m7	E♯m7♭5
B	Bmaj7	Emaj7	F♯7	C♯m7	D♯m7	G♯m7	A♯m7♭5
E	Emaj7	Amaj7	B7	F♯m7	G♯m7	C♯m7	D♯m7♭5
A	Amaj7	Dmaj7	E7	Bm7	C♯m7	F♯m7	G♯m7♭5
D	Dmaj7	Gmaj7	A7	Em7	F♯m7	Bm7	C♯m7♭5
G	Gmaj7	Cmaj7	D7	Am7	Bm7	Em7	F♯m7♭5

Minor Keys (Used for Minor Blues, Rock and R&B):

Note: The V chord is given as a dominant seventh because the dominant seventh has a much stronger tendency to resolve to the i chord, but you may use a minor seventh chord in its place. You may also use a minor seventh chord in place of a ii7♭5 chord.

	Primary chords			*Secondary chords*			
Key	**i**	**iv**	**V**	**ii**	**III**	**VI**	**VII**
C	Cm7	Fm7	G7	Dm7♭5	E♭maj7	A♭maj7	B♭7
F	Fm7	B♭m7	C7	Gm7♭5	A♭maj7	D♭maj7	E♭7
B♭	B♭m7	E♭m7	F7	Cm7♭5	D♭maj7	G♭maj7	A♭7
E♭	E♭m7	A♭m7	B♭7	Fm7♭5	G♭maj7	C♭maj7	D♭7
A♭	A♭m7	D♭m7	E♭7	B♭m7♭5	C♭maj7	F♭maj7	G♭7
C♯ (D♭)	C♯m7	F♯m7	G♯7	D♯m7♭5	Emaj7	Amaj7	B7
F♯	F♯m7	Bm7	C♯7	G♯m7♭5	Amaj7	Dmaj7	E7
B	Bm7	Em7	F♯7	C♯m7♭5	Dmaj7	Gmaj7	A7
E	Em7	Am7	B7	F♯m7♭5	Gmaj7	Cmaj7	D7
A	Am7	Dm7	E7	Bm7♭5	Cmaj7	Fmaj7	G7
D	Dm7	Gm7	A7	Em7♭5	Fmaj7	B♭maj7	C7
G	Gm7	Cm7	D7	Am7♭5	B♭maj7	E♭maj7	F7

Fingerboard Diagrams Showing the Location of Chords

The following diagrams show you the location of all of the notes of all four types of triads, all four types of seventh chords, the three types of ninth chords, and dominant thirteenth chords. All of the examples are given in the key of C. The purpose of these diagrams is to help you see how all the voicings fit together and to help you find them. The altered chords, eleventh chords, and chords from Chapter 10 (Other Chords) are not given. I recommend you make your own diagrams for these remaining chords and for the remaining keys.

C Major Triad - Over Entire Fingerboard

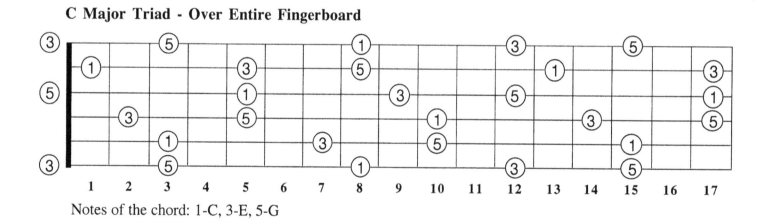

Notes of the chord: 1-C, 3-E, 5-G

C Minor Triad - Over Entire Fingerboard

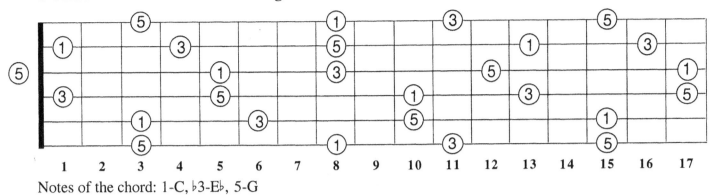

Notes of the chord: 1-C, ♭3-E♭, 5-G

C Diminished Triad - Over Entire Fingerboard

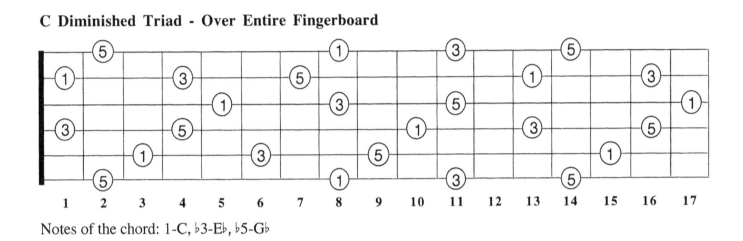

Notes of the chord: 1-C, ♭3-E♭, ♭5-G♭

C Augmented Triad - Over Entire Fingerboard

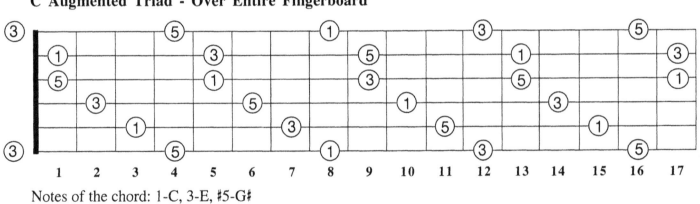

Notes of the chord: 1-C, 3-E, ♯5-G♯

C Major 7th Chord - Over Entire Fingerboard

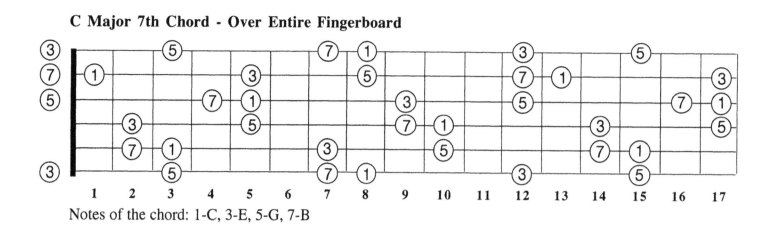

Notes of the chord: 1-C, 3-E, 5-G, 7-B

C Dominant 7th Chord - Over Entire Fingerboard

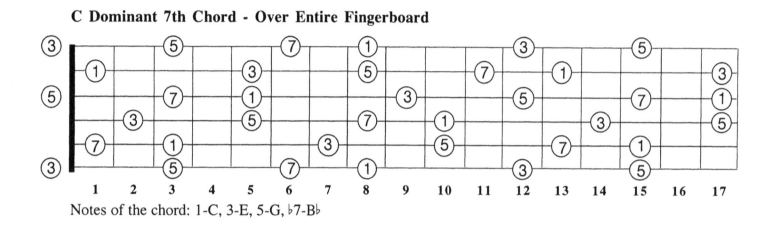

Notes of the chord: 1-C, 3-E, 5-G, ♭7-B♭

C Minor 7th Chord - Over Entire Fingerboard

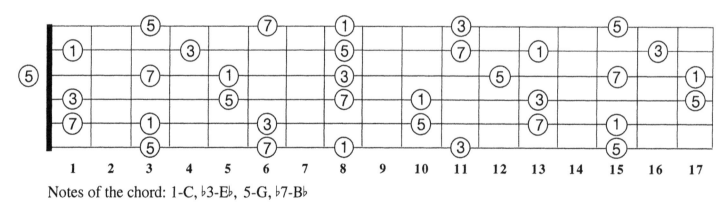

Notes of the chord: 1-C, ♭3-E♭, 5-G, ♭7-B♭

C Diminished 7th Chord - Over Entire Fingerboard

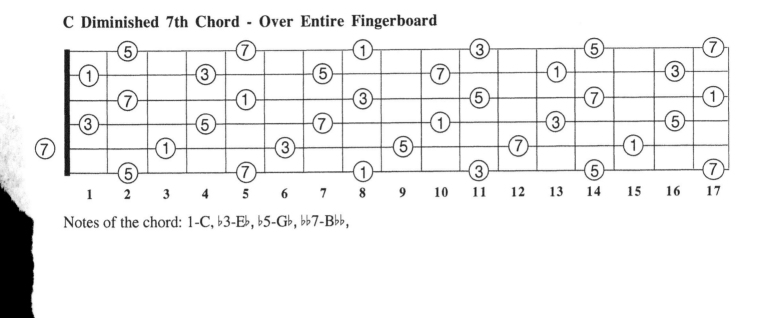

Notes of the chord: 1-C, ♭3-E♭, ♭5-G♭, ♭♭7-B♭♭,

C Major 6th Chord - Over Entire Fingerboard

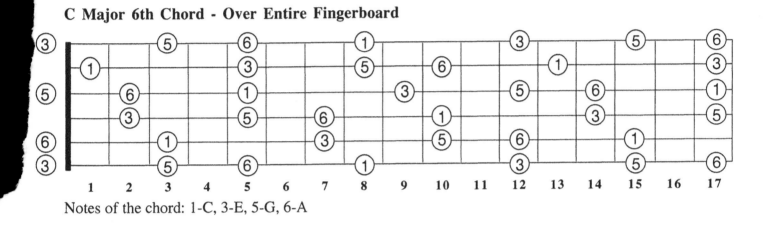

Notes of the chord: 1-C, 3-E, 5-G, 6-A

C Major 9th Chord - Over Entire Fingerboard

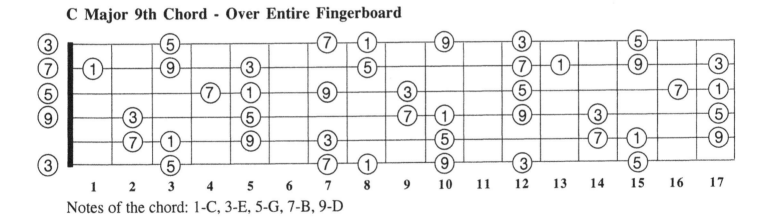

Notes of the chord: 1-C, 3-E, 5-G, 7-B, 9-D

C Dominant 9th Chord - Over Entire Fingerboard

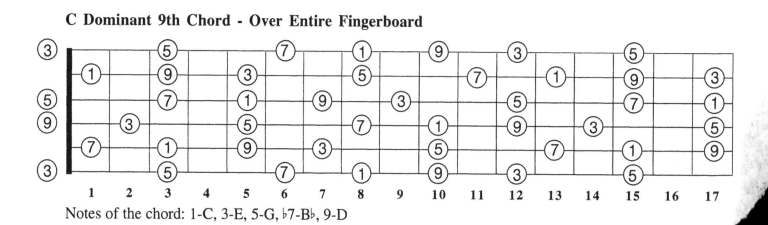

Notes of the chord: 1-C, 3-E, 5-G, ♭7-B♭, 9-D

C Minor 9th Chord - Over Entire Fingerboard

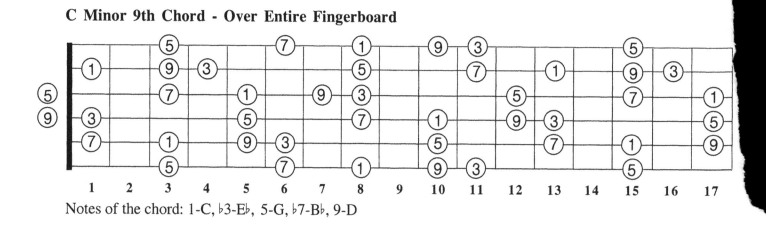

Notes of the chord: 1-C, ♭3-E♭, 5-G, ♭7-B♭, 9-D

C Dominant 13th Chord - Over Entire Fingerboard

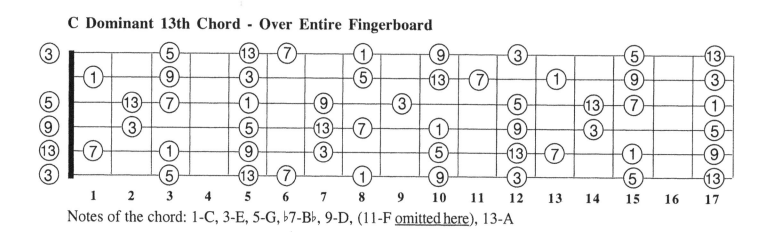

Notes of the chord: 1-C, 3-E, 5-G, ♭7-B♭, 9-D, (11-F omitted here), 13-A

120